C000117289

LOCK,

STOCK AND

TWO

SMOKING

PAELLAS

By

E.J. WOOD

Cover design by Black Cat Books

LOCK, STOCK AND TWO SMOKING PAELLAS

Black Cat Books

Lock, Stock and Two Smoking Paellas by E.J. Wood

1st edition

ALSO BY E.J. WOOD

Amalie

The Kidnapper's Word

The Boy in the Box

Beyond the Pale

The Forgotten Man

This book is dedicated to my husband, Mark. Thank you for joining me on this miraculous journey and encouraging me to continue writing, because I know while I'm out of your hair, it's truly what makes you happy.
This story would not exist if it wasn't for you.
To many more good times.

And there I marvelled at the forest's trees; my soul rooted to its deep verdant sea.
I could no more leave it, than it could walk from me.

ANGIE WEILAND-CROSBY

"AL MAL TIEMPO, BUENA CARA"
(Even if things go wrong, put on a brave face)

It was the day I gazed at Calpe beach that I saw a couple of people placing their towels over beach chairs before heading into the water. This was their way of claiming their spot on the over-crowded beach. It made me wonder if they had crawled bollock naked across hot coals to snag a special travel deal to get here. Regardless of the weather, they were determined to enjoy their time on the Costa Blanca and take a dip in the sea.

And thus was born the idea of Lock, Stock and Two Smoking Paellas. Before you delve into this book, here's what you should know. If you are looking to learn about Spain's picturesque beaches, rich history and delectable cuisine, this book might not be the right fit for you. In fact, it might even dissuade you from visiting Spain altogether. But then again, it might just pique your curiosity and inspire you to explore this beautiful country.

However, I can offer some interesting insights into the country's culture and traditions. For instance, did you know that Spain is home to the world's largest food fight festival? Known as *La Tomatina* – The battle of the tomatoes. This event takes place in the town of Buñol, near Valencia on the last Wednesday of August every year.

Nearly 20,000 people attend this colourful and emblematic event, where they hurl around one hundred and thirty tonnes of tomatoes at each other, just for fun!

It has an interesting history behind it, too. It all started in 1945 when a group of young people tried to disrupt the procession of another festival. In response, an angry crowd started throwing vegetables from a nearby stall, and the boys returned the following year with their own tomatoes to repeat the altercation. Despite various attempts by police to dissolve the tradition, La Tomatina has become a beloved and enduring part of Spanish culture.

The event was prohibited in the 1950s, but it didn't stop *La Tomatina*, and some people were even arrested for throwing tomatoes at each other.

However, due to public outcry, leaders were forced to accept it as an official festival. Although Buñol isn't too far away from us now, I could think of better things to do with my free time than get covered in tomato juice, and end up with a couple of black eyes, because not everyone crushes their tomatoes before they throw them. Nevertheless, tickets sell out immediately.

I have been living in the Valencian region on the east coast of Spain for nearly thirty years, so it can't be all bad, right? The Spanish certainly know how to enjoy life, and maybe they can teach me a lesson or two. Then again, if I haven't learnt anything yet, I doubt there's any hope for me! However, I do feel the need to let my hair down, so to speak. It's been long enough that I've called this country my home.

Nevertheless, one thing I've learnt is that life certainly is a learning curve, often hurling boulders in our path. But we must make the most of it, embrace it, and enjoy every moment. After all, we only have one life to live. That's what I try to tell myself. However, sometimes it can be overwhelming and get the better of me. You know what they say: *when life gives you lemons, make lemonade.*

My name is Abbie. I know what you're thinking: "She must speak Spanish." Well, I'll give you the same answer I give everyone else: I don't speak English. Cue nervous laughter. Let's be honest, do any of us know every word in the English language? I certainly don't. The topic of language in Spain is quite controversial and varies depending on the region you reside in. The country has four co-official languages: Catalan (a Romance language spoken in eastern and northeastern Spain), Basque, Galician/Galego (spoken in Galicia and neighbouring regions such as Asturias, Castile and León), and Aranese (a Pyrenean Gascon language spoken in the Val d'aran in northwestern Catalonia.). Or perhaps you mean Spanish *Spanish* when you ask if I speak Spanish? Let's not forget the local dialect Valenciano...

Español or as it is known around the rest of the Spanish-speaking world is *Castellano (Castillian),* it is the official name given by the Spanish Constitution of 1978. And it defines the official language for the whole of Spain.

I was born in Britain but raised in Spain, and even after thirty years, I still find myself surprised by the people, animals, the country itself – not always in a good way. Spain has a dark side that is often overlooked. Despite having traveled extensively, I find myself drawn back to Spain time and time again. Perhaps it's the warm climate, the natural environment, or the colourful and rich ambiance.

I first met Mark Davies over a decade ago. He was a charming, self-confessed know-it-all who apparently looked like Phil Vickery *(English Celebrity chef)* and was an all-around arse-wipe. I, on the other hand, am certainly no Fern Britton.

This isn't a story about our joyous adventure in uprooting from one country to another and having a ball of a time. No, and if that's what you're looking for, then this book isn't for you.

I met Mark soon after he arrived in Spain. Initially, he had a tough time adjusting to the new environment after moving from the UK.

I tried to help him appreciate the little things that make us smile, the oddities such as the locals randomly greeting each other on the street or inviting us to join their table even though no one spoke English.

Nowadays, Mark and the Spanish locals converse in a combination of nods, smiles and Spanglish. In our experience, the local people are very welcoming, especially in rural areas. This was a welcome surprise to Mark, who is still shocked at the generosity of strangers.

This is our story, with no airs and graces; we're not sugarcoating anything. Living in Spain is not all sun, sea and sand. Sometimes it's more manure than roses. Our story is punctuated with domestics, lots of bad language, and on occasion, laughs. I've also included a couple of useful recipes, some of which you can easily prepare when living off-grid with no refrigerator or electricity. Additionally, I've added some hamtastic tapa suggestions for when you're out dining.

We've evolved a philosophy that works for us,

one that allows us to live relatively cheaply and happily, often referring to ourselves as rich, not in a monetary way, but rich in our souls.

We're not the luckiest people going, and if something could go wrong, it did and still does. Coupled with Mark's outbursts of profanity, (OK, mine too), reluctant farmers, persistent and savage insects, and ravenous wild animals, we began to wonder why we ever made the decision to leave everything we had come to know behind on the coast for a fresh start renovating a finca in the countryside where we can count kilometers to socially distance.

Our relationship has survived until now, and our 90s Land Rover keeps going despite what the rumours say; 90% of Land Rovers are still on the road, and the other 10% made it to their destination. So what more could test our patience? And will we ever find our happily ever after in the Spanish countryside?

PROLOGUE

Just one bullet

Mark gulped a can of Coca Cola, and stared out of the car window. I could see in his eyes he was, in this very moment, contemplating how we came about the circumstances we found ourselves in, but the truth of the matter was that the reality of the situation was far different than it appeared. I sighed deeply as we waited. It was almost 9 o'clock at night, according to the digital display in the old Land Rover, and the night started to draw to a close. At this time of the year, it didn't get dark until about now, so we hung on so we could venture out under the cloak of darkness before we departed the vehicle. Waiting patiently, we silently observed, careful not to draw any attention to ourselves - two Brits sitting ominously in their car. Time had never stood still for so long nor been so quiet. It was deafening.

We weren't given many instructions, just to be here, today, a Tuesday evening at 9 o'clock. Other than that, we didn't know what to expect. We'd already waited half an hour, not wanting to be late. The saying goes if you're on time then you're already late, and this wasn't someone we wanted to start off on the wrong foot with.

The clouds loomed overhead, casting ominous shadows on the ground below. The distant rumble of thunder signaled the impending arrival of rain. As the first drops began to fall, I quickly wound up my window, bracing myself for the heavy downpour that would soon follow. The sound of raindrops pounding against the aluminium roof of our agricultural vehicle filled the air, as we continued our wait through the stormy weather.

Mark slowly and quietly unlatched his seatbelt, readjusting his position in the car. He hoped that our movements would not attract the attention of any unsuspecting passerby outside the small bar nearby. The bar was integrated into townhouses on either side. Tables were out the front with chairs pulled forward and leaning against them. A bright purple Bougainvillea plant strangled the metal framework in front of the sole window, while a couple of men stood outside puffing on cigarettes. It was a dismal sight, and neither of us was interested in visiting the bar, especially since we didn't drink alcohol.

Yet the gloomy bar appeared to beckon the local patrons and sucked them into its depression. Spanish bars rarely had any atmosphere; bright LED lights like an old school canteen. When the men finished their cigarettes, they squeezed back into the crowded bar. The deafening drone was inescapable. We had heard rumours the bar was *the* place to go, you know, if you *had* to meet someone. Associated with illegal activities, everyone just kept their heads down and stayed out of everyone's business – we had come to learn that it was the way in small villages, so that's what we did.

As our eyes watched the crowd, a man over 6ft tall and heavy build caught our attention. He skulked towards the entrance of the bar, hunched over with his hands in pockets. Immediately we sensed that this was probably who we were waiting for. He certainly looked like he was capable of more than mere violence. *"Just don't look at his eyes, he doesn't like that."* we were warned.

'You're having a laugh aren't you?' I replied at the time.

'He usually comes in around 9 o'clock, but I didn't tell you. Got it?' the server had said as she looked side to side over her shoulders.

The man in question was called Pedro, at least, that's the name we were given. That's all we were told – the guy to go to if you wanted something sourced and dispatched. He wasn't the typical suit-wearing type that we're used to seeing in movies, real killers are rarely suave, and I've never known one to wear a suit –not that I've met many killers. This guy was a greasy, pot-bellied Spaniard that you wouldn't want to meet down a dark alley that's for sure. There were plenty like him around and he blended in perfectly.

'Let's get this over and done with, Mark,' I sighed as we exited the car. 'Let me do the talking.'

Mark still didn't speak much Spanish, but with his olive skin and dark hair, no one would know.

'We don't want you saying *si* and agreeing to something too sinister, all right? From what the waitress told us, this guy has a reputation of being especially brutal, easily lifting a 260lbs corpse over his shoulder,' I reminded him.

'Abbie, when it comes to money, I leave the negotiating up to you.'

CHAPTER 1

Stop wining…

Six months before.

'I didn't move to Spain just to slog my guts off!' Mark exclaimed as we drove along the tarmac road in our 90s Land Rover, heading towards our local *cafetería* on the Spanish coast. I remember the day well; the sun was shining, as it usually does in sunny Spain, and there was a beautiful crisp clarity to the fields of vines.

'And you think I did? To listen to an old fart moaning all the time?' I retorted. It wasn't uncommon for us to bicker at some point during the day because, truth be told, we were both sick and tired of the way things were. Over the years, our bickering had turned into more of a comedy act, and friends and family relished in our offering of light entertainment. *How to survive living and working with someone 24/7.*

I had already been living in Spain for over a decade when Mark and I met, so naturally, I became his go-to translator. The only thing he managed to retain was "*café con leche, por favor*," despite my efforts to teach him more. I would like to say he tried, but he didn't. In all honesty, when he did try back in the early days, he would drop the most outrageous vernacular blunders that it almost felt safer just to take over. Accented letters in Spanish are vital in pronouncing words that are spelt the same as others. For example, you would want to say *'Soy inglés,'* when telling someone that you're English, not *'Soy ingles,'* which means "I'm the groin." And if it's hot outside, make sure to say, *'Tengo calor'* or *'Hace calor,'* because fanning your face and saying, '*¡Estoy caliente!*' meaning "I'm horny" will be sure to garner you a few laughs - even though *caliente* does indeed translate to hot.

By this time, meeting Mark, I hadn't visited much of the country despite my years living here. Nor did I realise I was living in one of the most prolific wine-producing areas. I had no idea that there was even global excitement at the very product the area produced – wine. I just grew up seeing hordes of tourists arrive by the coach load from Benidorm getting pissed up on free samples offered at the local bodegas. Nothing said summer had arrived like seeing lobster-coloured tourists man-handling gallons of wine under each armpit, their tight vests and waving fans. As we drove into town, fields of olive and almond trees adorned either side of the road. The beautiful pink and white blossom that had been out in full bloom were now slowly disappearing as the heat penetrated the sky.

It was a Saturday morning, and the local flea market more commonly known as the *rastro* was being held; an overpriced secondhand market selling bric-a-brac, and any old crap you'd usually throw out. One man's trash is another man's treasure, they say. However, the tourists love it. It was probably one of the only things that remained unchanged since I moved to Spain, it's just got bigger, and the crap crappier. So much in this once small village has changed.

Changing the subject, I asked, 'Are we popping in to see your mother?' I knew that we could count on finding toast and peanut butter in her fridge, even if it was slightly past its expiration date. During one of her house moves, I helped my mother-in-law pack up her belongings and discovered three-year-old frozen turkeys in her chest freezer. When I asked her about it, she explained that during the war, food was scarce, so she never threw anything away. Even though we remind her that she didn't actually experience the war, we can always count on her to have a well-stocked fridge. Good old mother-in-law. We'll never go hungry with her around.

'Give her a ring and see if she's in,' he snapped.

'Are you going to be in a bad mood all day?' I shook my head. He didn't answer.

'Do you want to go back to the UK, or do you really want to stay here with me?' I asked knowing it would provoke an instant retraction.

'No way do I want to go back to the UK. Spain has many faults, but I wouldn't go back to the UK, too friggin´ cold for starters, and stop asking if I want to stay with you. We've been through far too much together,' he answered determinedly.

'We agree on something then!'

We passed a line of mules towing beaten up carriages, and behind the carriages a tractor tyre. Even a Jack Russell panted at the back trying to keep pace. *Why they didn't just pop him on the back I'll never know...poor bugger*, I thought. Seeing the gypsy carriages and horses through town admittedly was different, but even by Spanish standards they really weren't that spectacular. I remember when I moved here, to the Vall de pop, that the renowned ex-bull keeper had a lion he used to parade around town. I never saw it with my own eyes; I moved out just after he stopped or it died, but it wouldn't surprise me – not with what I've seen. As we overtook the carriages and headed towards the mother-in-law's, we passed the *Mercat de la Terra* – a farmer's market held in conjunction with the flea market. The market faces the riverbed and is renowned for its craftwork and fresh produce. One of the most popular items sold here is *Queso Tetilla,* a cheese that is shaped like a double D cup breast, hence the name 'tit'. You can also find a wide variety of *embutido* (Spanish cured cold meat and sausages) here.

Throughout Spain, local markets often offer samples of cured meats that stallholders are eager to hand out to entice customers to purchase their artisanal delicacies. In addition, there is an abundance of fresh, seasonal, local produce such as strawberries and cherries available here. So, forget about the less desirable supermarket produce with post-harvesting treatments and head over to this market for a delightful shopping experience.

We drove through the pandemonium; visitors crossing the road willy-nilly, Mark shouting expletives.

'*GRACIAS. DE NADA*. Ignorant bastards.' Maybe a change wasn't a bad idea. I thought quietly. It's not that I disliked the area, because the coast, and its little valleys are beautiful, but I'm a country girl at heart, and the area had changed so much in so few years that both Mark and I were still imbued with the idea of how Spain was twenty years ago, before tourism took over. Now, on the coast, you'd be lucky if you could walk down the road without hearing someone speak English. Not being able to speak Spanish really isn't an issue anymore depending on where you move to.

When I first moved to Spain, I couldn't buy a packaged chicken in the supermarket like you would expect from Tescos or Sainsburys – you had to go to the meat counter or a butcher, and ask for a *pollo limpio;* which translated to a clean chicken, because back then, the meat had been dispatched but it still had feathers. And let's be clear, that is pollo not polla: Not to be mistaken by many newcomers who receive raised eyebrows when asking for a clean penis.

I still remember how Spain was when I first moved here; of course not speaking a word of Spanish and thinking the corner shop emblazoned with the word FERRETERIA was some kind of ghoulish, satanic shop with a tarot reader and a dead, stuffed ferret sitting on her shoulder.

Nevertheless, if you do find yourself on the Spanish coast, do visit the cave paintings. We frequently passed the Pla de Petracos in Castell de Castells on our motorcycle rideouts. They're known as Neolithic art, and they're huge and exceptional and appear untouched. They were created by the peasant people during the Neolithic period, and

UNESCO *(United Nations Educational, Scientific and Cultural Organization)* has declared it as a World Heritage site. Despite many tourists staying in coastal towns near to the area such as Javeá, the public remains unaware of its existence. A must-see for prehistory enthusiasts.

To get there from Castell de Castells, take the long, sweeping road towards Benichembla. About five kilometers from the village of Castell de Castells, turn left to a track to the Barranco where the paintings are.

However, if you head towards North West Spain, don't miss the impressive Archaeological site of Atapuerca; where actual fossils of hominids have been found. There is also a Museum of Human Evolution in Burgos city. Head further West and you'll jump through time, ending up in Galicia where remains of the Iron Age and hill forts from the 6th century. It's amazing what's out there.

So here we were on our way to my mother-in-law's place. What a force to be reckoned with she is, and she is confident to put me in my place whenever she feels like it. Sheila had been living in Spain for nearly fifteen years, having moved out after a messy divorce back in the UK. Now, she is eighty-four going on twenty-five, and behaves like a bull in a china shop. Ironic when her house is full of Lladró. She is one of life's phenomenon's, still partying in Benidorm til 6 o'clock in the morning, getting married, widowed and now with a new boyfriend eleven years her junior. There just really isn't any stopping her. Built like a carthorse, she and her friend Maria would traipse up and down the high street shopping, because there is always a deal somewhere, where the shop will double the sale price, and then say it's on sale with a discount of 20%. *Yes, we know you all do it.* Sheila had managed to surround herself with a huge expat community, because she too didn't speak a word of Spanish even after fifteen years. Whether they wanted her around or not, she is the life, soul, and center of any party; she loves life, and at her age why would we stop her?

As I walked through her front door, I greeted her in my usual fashion. 'Hi, Sheila, is everything all right?'

'Hello, Darling. Wanna cuppa?' she beamed.

'Silly question,' I nod.

'Where is he?' she asked as she looked at the front door.

'He's coming. He's in a mood.'

'Again?'

'Again….'

'Oh for fuck's sake…' she murmured.

It always did make me laugh how she reprimanded me for swearing when she had the dirtiest potty mouth amongst us. She would strongly disagree – of course.

'Hi, Mom,' Mark said as he sat beside me.

'Any news?'

'Just more lying estate agents,' he shrugged.

'Oh shit,' she swore again as she placed two cups of tea in front of us.

'What about you, done anything new lately?' he asked.

'I went out shopping with Maria.'

'Did she bring the dog?' he smiled.

Sheila didn't particularly like the dog in question, a teacup Chihuahua whose sole purpose in life was to be Maria's pacifier.

'Yes…no one likes it. I keep telling her she cannot bring it. It's like a rat. It's getting to the point I'm just going to plain refuse to be seen out in public with her. Fucking thing is always snapping, bark, bark, snap, snap, it's like it's her baby.'

'But with teeth…' I interrupted.

'Yes, always in her handbag. The bloody thing won't even go outside to shit.' Sheila stood up reenacting the placement of a piece of kitchen roll. 'It shits on this,' she growls squatting over the square sheet of paper.

'Oh that's not nice,' I smirk.

'I know. And she takes it into restaurants, and all you get is it shoved in everyone's face. I'm sure she does it for the attention.'

'Well, at the end of the day she's happy and it really is quite adorable,' he laughed. 'It's smaller than our cats.'

'You never have been an animal lover though, have you, Sheila?' I declare.

'I love animals, just don't want them around me,' she answered, and Mark and I looked at one another.

Sheila's house was situated in a quiet town; I call it God's waiting room because the average age seemed to be about seventy-five, and everyone around that age just sits outside the church staring into space. Nevertheless, her house had a beautiful view. Just over the pool edge we could look down onto groves of lemon and orange trees, as well as copious vines. If I squinted, I could see farmers bottoms up gathering buckets of grapes, the odd tractor ploughing, and machinery driving towards the Bodegas with hoards of grapes.

The bright, yellow sun pierced through the glass conservatory, and I seated myself comfortably.

'Well...go on then...' she urged. 'Tell me about your latest property viewings.' Her question distracted me from looking down towards the pool where a couple of years ago she had slipped, knocking herself unconscious on the pool edge, and if it wasn't for the exceptional Spanish health service she might not have survived.

'You'll need to put the kettle on first,' I laughed.

CHAPTER 2

You'll be alright if you always assume the estate agent is lying.

When I reflect on it, I would prefer to get straight to the point of where we actually ended up buying. However, there were far too many noteworthy properties that, to be honest, if I didn't write it down, no one would believe me. You still might not.

Our property search has been on and off for the

past five years, and we pretty much started to lose hope of ever finding our dream home. Especially when realised we wasted time viewing a property that had the upstairs converted into an area with tens of canary cages that hung from wooden beams and gaps in the rooftop.

Our noteworthy mentions started about four years ago when we were told about a property that had been featured on a British television show about unscrupulous and incompetent builders who take peoples' money and ruin lives. When we told the mother-in-law, she sat there with a face that looked like it had frozen in time.

The story of the dilapidated old farmhouse came about when a couple emigrated from England to Spain with the dream of opening a hotel. Unfortunately, their fortune ran out when they met local con-artist and property developer Dodgy Sam. You see, Dodgy Sam had been operating in the area for well over twenty years, and his reputation preceded him. He knew the law inside out – he even managed to rip off friends of Sheila for fifty grand, as well as many others.

Mark and I looked at one of his properties and found out it had a well, but there was no license to withdraw water from it. Additionally, the property had a demolition order against it. But *"Don't worry,"* he said, *"they'll never tear it down."* Not a risk we were willing to take. To be honest, with his parading around town in a colourful Lamborghini, it's a wonder he hadn't had his legs broken.

The other couple however, invested nearly a million euro, only to be told a few weeks later, they too needed an operating license, and were subsequently shut down, having believed that investing such an amount that the licence would have been "thrown in". That and the rising sewage that passed through the garden didn't make for an enjoyable stay around the hotel pool – that's dodgy building practices, and that's another subject. We viewed the property some fifteen years later, after this incident. By now, it looked like bombed out Beirut. Squatters and gypsies had helped themselves to every door, window and copper piping. But for us – it was just what we were looking for and, more importantly, it was at the right price. Of course, one of our first appointments had been with the village's mayor to make sure it was possible to get the necessary licences to carry out the works needed.

Our fiasco went on for about six months dealing with the bank that now had possession. In the meantime, roof tiles were disappearing by the dozen. Mark and I spent much of our free time going to and fro to this property, devastated that with each visit there was visibly more damage. We spent hours photographing and documenting the changes over the course of six months, in the hope the bank would hurry the process along or at the very least reduce the asking price.

One evening as it wore on, Mark professed to

wanting to catch the vandals red handed. I looked at him in angst but took him up on the offer of side-kick like Batman and Robin. We parked up a few hundred meters away, and with us dressed in black and a couple of items for self protection, there was very little chance anyone would hear us coming as we navigated through the dark woods listening to only the nocturnal sounds of the surrounding fauna. A small, yellow light flickered from the upstairs room. We crept inside, me covering the back, Mark poking his head around the corner of every room and whispering, 'Clear.' Our years of Airsoft and military simulation gaming finally paying off. We ascended the stairs, entered the room, assumed position, cleared corners and one by one secured the upstairs rooms. One room was dimly lit, and we saw from the door way an eerie shadow. My heart raced as we cautiously stepped inside. I breathed deep, catching the breath in my throat and my mind ran wild with the terrifying possibility we were both going to get kidnapped or beaten up. Mark stepped in front of me, the sound magnified and amplified my anxiety, but I couldn't let him go in alone. Together, panic washed over us as we saw two people squatting in the corner and they screamed. The two young, love-struck teenagers screamed with their heart and soul.

'DON'T HURT US!' the girl trembled.

'English? For fuck's sake, get out of here,' Mark sighed.

We doubted they were our vandals, instead, opportunistic youths now terrified for their lives.

'This is ridiculous,' I said as I removed my mask. 'We cannot carry on like this; it's taking over our lives. The outcome could have been far worse.'

'Yes. They could have set the place ablaze,' he agreed.

'I meant with whom we would have found. We could have been stuffed into the back of someone's boot or knifed.'

'Don't be ridiculous,' he laughed.

Nevertheless, the thefts continued. Evidence illustrated that gypsies of a foreign nationality were present most days using the cloak of darkness to carry out their sinister actions. Tyre tracks where they loaded up their van with roof tiles, and therefore exposed the underlying roof to the elements. The restoration budget was on the increase, so Mark donned his large, black puffer jacket, and we walked into the only bar in the village. Mark claimed he had contacts and was a member of a well-known biker gang, and we were the prospective buyers. The barmen chuckled, that was until every other punter walked out and Mark's unwavering, intense and prolonged gaze made him realise we weren't messing around.

Police wouldn't be interested in such a menial report of things going missing in an open and derelict property so sometimes you just have to take things into your own hands. Suffice to say, several days later, we noticed a large pile of roof tiles were piled up by the entrance. Yet, the bank just fobbed us off until they told us it was sold. We found out a while later – to the mayor's son…

So with broken hearts we continued our search, this time, with the philosophy of not allowing our house-hunt to turn into an obsession.

'They say good things come to those that wait,' Mark shrugged.

'Those that are patient.'

Unfortunately, our experience with repossessed properties had not ended. Our new property of interest was 600m2 (6500sft) on two floors.

'*Todo legal*,' All legal the estate agent said.

'This is more like it; at least it has windows, even if they are cracked.' I smiled as we walked around the garden.

'It's by a motorway,' Mark said disappointingly.

'But you don't hear it. It's remarkably quiet considering.'

The monumental building and ancient trees gave us a new spark, a new hope, a vision of all things possible, until we found out it wasn't legal, had no electric, and wouldn't likely ever do so because no certificate of habitation would be issued. So, with this knowledge, the bank doubled the asking price.

'It's time we started looking further afield. With the pittance we've saved, we're never going to find anywhere other than a cow shed.' Mark dropped his head in despair.

'Even cows wouldn't live in some of these properties. Look,' I asked as I showed Mark a few more properties that had popped into my email inbox.

Charming casita for sale, a bijou bolt-hole of 17sqm built to a high standard. Fenced 2,500sqm plot…

'What's a bijou bolt-hole?' he crinkled his face.

'Well, bijou means jewel, something small, delicate or dainty, 17sqm of escapism?'

'A small, but attractive place to escape to?'

'I suppose so,' I nodded.

'Why don't they just say that then instead of using big words,' he shrugged. 'Besides, what are you going to do in 17sqm, play spin the bottle?'

'You shouldn't laugh; there are smaller apartments in New York.'

As Mark stood up to go to the bathroom his mother stood up and grabbed my arm.

'That reminds me, dear…Mark's birthday.'

'We're not going to be celebrating it; we're skint, and besides, with everything that is going on it wouldn't be any fun.'

'But we must do something.' Sheila had broached the subject before, her approach was an adroitly circuitous route, and not unlike the time she came up to the workshop, pulled a pair of red, laced knickers from her handbag, and said I should wear them for her son on Valentine's Day. I'm not sure what was more mortifying; my mother-in-law buying me knickers or that the tag had XL. I whipped them from her clutches and shoved them under my top. *'I was cleaning out my bottom drawer…'*

'Oh…' I gasped.

'So,' she whispered whilst Mark was in the bathroom. 'Mark's birthday: Maybe we'll go for a curry.'

'Sounds like a plan.'

Mark walked into the room, 'Did I miss anything?' he asked as I burst into laughter.

'No, I was just telling your mum about where we went last week.'

'Oh, the dog shit place,' he shook his head.

'Right…'

'Dog shit? I'll put the kettle back on. Anyone for a chocolate biscuit?'

'Go on then.' Mark replied, then leant over towards me and asked what was so funny.

I whispered, 'Your mum blew off as she got up, again…' Mark shook his head and tutted. 'She's got a real problem.'

Sheila popped her head round the corner, 'What about you, dear? Chocolate biscuit?'

'I won't, thank you, Sheila. I have to watch my weight. Fight the flab and all.'

'Don't be so stupid, there's nothing of you,' she retorted.

Mark smiled. 'You know what Dad always said;

skip to melt the fat off.' Mark smiled remembering his late father who had recently passed away.

'You're not helping. I will never be a stickleback, much to your disappointment…' I scowled.

Sheila shook her head, 'Stickleback?'

'It's a spiny fish.'

Sheila disregarded the explanation.

'Why are you laughing, Abbie?' Sheila crinkled her brows and Mark interjected.

'Because you farted…again! You should be careful with all these candles; you could set the place on fire.'

Sheila chuckled.

'You don't fart in front of your new boyfriend do you?' Mark referred to a time when his mother was dating a flash American pilot back in the early days. They had all gone out for a meal, and everything was going great, until Sheila let loose. Suffice it to say, the duo never saw one another again.

'I still don't know why you want to move so far away. Abbie, this is all you have known. Don't you like it here anymore?' Sheila asked.

'Of course!' I exclaimed. 'But it's exactly that. We just want change. Most British people who move out to Spain want the coast – they want the sun, sea and sand. But this is my home, I'm not a tourist.'

'We also want to be completely off-grid, like a homestead,' stated Mark.

'What's that mean?' Sheila queried.

'No electric or water bills, plus we want to grow our own vegetables.'

'Oh right. Hey, Abbie, you'll have to watch out with those small villages, I bet there isn't a lot of choice. The women will be looking at stealing Mark away,' Sheila concluded. I could feel myself busting with eye-rolling what-the-f's. Sheila found her son incredibly attractive, often commenting inappropriately if she was thirty years younger and all. Although, I'm sure she meant someone else, not her son, because it wasn't unlike Sheila to combine one conversation with another as her discursive speech was hard to follow, often jumping from one topic to another without any form of connection.

Maybe it was her age.

CHAPTER 3

There are just some places on the human body that Coca Cola bottles, giant candles and light bulbs should not go.

The Spanish countryside and its verdant valleys were areas of Spain that people never think about. It's almost always about the sun. Especially if you head down south – it's so barren. El Campello is not really considered southern Spain, and even then El Campello has a Wild West themed film set where tumbleweeds are not stage props. It's rugged, wild and barren.

When I first moved to Spain, it was all about making sure you returned home with a sombrero, a straw donkey, a Spanish fan or castanets. Nevertheless, if you venture further out from the coastal areas, you will find what I believe to be authentic Spain, at least the Spain as I remembered it some twenty odd years ago. Where the further inland you go means the further back in time you go and surprisingly you will be blown away with the traditional local cuisine you just don't find on the coast. If you are not bothered about your traditional English fish and chips, you can truly immerse yourself into a more traditional way of life. You won't find any Irish bars in the countryside. In addition, property prices are vastly different; you can get twice the house for half the price in the countryside, and in some parts of Spain even whole villages for less than 100k.

'You would love it, Sheila. We've seen some stunning scenery,' I smiled.

'Bit quiet for me,' she answered. 'What have you got planned for Christmas?'

'That's a bit far off…' Mark scoffed.

'We're going to Benidorm Palace,' Sheila said.

Mark interjected. 'Again? We are hoping to have our own home by then. Abbie is determined to put a tree up this year. Bless her.'

'I think you're both so brave. I admire you two,' Sheila held up her cup as if to toast us. 'I cannot wait to see what you get.'

Sheila enjoyed the nightlife, even at eighty-four.

We all lived about twenty minutes from Denia, a cosmopolitan town located halfway between Alicante and Valencia along the northern part of the Mediterranean coastline. It is famously known for its marina of 546 moorings, its beaches, history and gastronomy. Denia is located at the foot of a hill which is crowned by a 16th century castle along with an archaeological museum. Walking through the main street, Denia offers an array of cafés and designer shops. It buzzes with nightlife as live music and restaurants situated on the sea front attract people far and wide, even through winter, where many restaurants and bars close in smaller, lesser occupied villages. Denia focuses on tourism as its main industry, and has done so since the 60s when manufacturing and processing raisins no longer became profitable. And if you love oysters you must try the Ostrarium Bar.

However, Denia hides a dark past. Denia was the ratline for Nazis fleeing Europe following the Second World War. Below the crystal waters, Denia's murky past reveals that Nazis settled along the Spanish coasts, and was the chosen spot for a high-ranking Sturmbannfuhrer (a Nazi party paramilitary rank equivalent to major) in the Waffen SS called Gerhard Bremer. After his conviction at the Nuremberg trials, he lived happily in Denia until his death in 1989. He became a local businessman, and built hotels during the birth of the Costa Blanca's tourism. Some Nazis felt so comfortable in Spain, they never felt the need to renounce their Nazi ideology and often they met up to celebrate Hitler's birth, April 20th at Casa Finita restaurant, a place hidden in the mountains of Les Rotes, that nowadays serves as a hotel.

A half hour drive will take you to Calpe. Nearly three thousand years old and famous for its beautiful beaches, the gigantic granite rock towering 600 meters high sat on its beach, and the abundant birdlife, make Calpe a well-known town on the Costa Blanca.

I remember when I first visited Spain, Calpe and its famous fish market was one of the first places my family visited. Restaurants along the sea front display their daily catch so you can choose your seafood and often have it cooked in front of you. Calpe is a fishing village, and the fish auction really is a must-see event, even if you don't like fish. And if you don't like fish, then you won't forget the pungent whiff that constantly permeates the air. Calpe's fleet of fishing boats arrive every day, selling fresh fish to the restaurants and the public, and near around 5:00pm lasting for about an hour and a half to two hours is the daily fish auction held at *Lonja de la Cofradia de Pescadores*. Boxes of fish are unloaded onto conveyor belts, passing buyers, and electronic screens display the information of each lot, including the name of the boat, its weight and opening bid. The building, decorated by large paintings representing Calpe's history and scenes of daily life is emblematic of the town; make the auction one of Calpe's most visited of Calpe's activities as well as its famous rock *El Peñon de Ifach* which Mark says looks like a giant tooth erupting from the sea.

I never have been a true fan of fish and shellfish. My family usually resorted to the below par offerings of local supermarkets. So, if you truly want to experience a great seafood dish, it has to be fresh. Look for bright eyes, a gleaming skin, and don't worry, slim is apparently a good indication of freshness. Nor should fish smell, and if you buy it from the fish market, try and cook it that day, I certainly noticed a huge difference. Calpe for me retains some of its history and tradition, and some archaeological findings can be found at the Ifach cliffs.

Peñón de Ifach of Calpe

However, the fish market of Calpe was too tedious for Sheila, and she wasn't interested that the Romans had established themselves as a sustainable colony whose main activity was trading dry and salted fish. She wanted to party, and what better place to let your hair down than Benidorm. If it wasn't for her osteoarthritis, she'd be volunteering to be Sticky Vicky's replacement.

Benidorm Palace is a night venue featuring spectacular live dinner shows that has been going since 1977. Now, it is an established prestigious party venue, which includes many great international music artists, ballets and renowned orchestras. I heard over one and a half thousand spectators arrived on their opening night. Fifty years on, I've never had a bad experience, the show and catering is top notch. However, Benidorm town is another story. It took me fifteen years before I had my first night out in Benidorm, blasphemous I know, even though it was famed for many reasons long before the TV Series; BENIDORM.

One evening, Mark's brother-in-law Steve had joined us for a night out. I wouldn't say he could really hold his drink – evident when we went to Benidorm Palace one year for Christmas, and he was convinced the cabaret dancers were waving at him as they can canned, leaving very little to the imagination with their risqué semi-nude, musical acts.

Instead, we headed to what's known as the

English Square – two guesses why. Full of crazy Stag & Hen do's from England that started their fun on the flight over. The loud and obnoxious partygoers are often found with a hired dwarf handcuffed to the stag. However, would you really have a good time if you weren't taken away in an ambulance, half naked, with a group of oompa loompas at your side? During Carnival in Benidorm, things could be worse.

Sticky Vicky's show is regarded as one of Benidorm's legendary acts. Her notoriously x-rated show shot her to fame in the 1980s, and she appeared as a guest of honour on the TV series: BENIDORM. Stupefied tourists are amazed and horrified as they see her pull out razor blades from, a place down-under where you wouldn't think to put a ping-pong ball, a bottle of beer much less a razor blade or anything else for that matter. Adding to the name *sticky*... Now retired, her daughter continues the famous performance, so do yourself a favour when you're next in Benidorm, and book yourself a room with a view…

Spain is mostly all I have known, and I genuinely do love living here, but don't get me wrong, there are a few grievances – their coffee being one of them. It can be a Spain in the butt, often served cold or at best, luke-warm. Too bitter for my taste too, but if you're wanting to try it and you're up for something that's a little more novelty than taste then try a *Carajillo*; a hot coffee cocktail using Brandy or Rum as the liquor of choice. If you're lucky, the bartender will set the alcohol on fire. If you're unlucky and greedy, you'll just burn yourself and singe a few eyebrows.

'We are lucky though, aren't we, Mark?' I asked. 'When you think about it, there are worse places to live.'

'I know, I'll just be happy when this stage of our life is over with.'

I agreed. 'It's something to look forward to, to sit in our own garden, listening to the cicadas, and sipping on Sangria.'

'If we ever get there,' Mark sighed.

The Spanish countryside

CHAPTER 4

The Dog Shit place

After 60 miles on the road, we had arrived in Canals. Sharing its borders with municipalities of l'Alcúdia de Crespins and many more, it is located in the valley of Montesa. In the 19th century Canals developed an industry with twenty-four glass factories, paper factories, metal workshops and flour mills, with *The Moli Vell* being one such factory. It had been acquired at auction by a property developer in 2018 and now was up for sale.

Surprisingly, the property wasn't actually called the dog shit place. That was just what we called it. It was in fact a 14th century flour mill situated in the Spanish countryside that ran alongside a canal. *How wonderful* we thought, our very own castle-esque house in Spain.

Before we undertook the journey, Mark and I beamed in delight. 'We've got to go and have a look at this one, it's huge,' Mark said enthusiastically.

'There's got to be a catch.' If it sounds too good to be true, it usually is.

'Worth a look though. If all else fails, we get a bike ride out of it,' he shrugged.

After being on the road for just over an hour, and Mark whipping in and out of traffic as if we were in an arcade video game, we stopped at the impressive old flour mill. Anyone else would have been certain of his or her imminent death. I had become accustomed to scream when airborne and laugh when the tyres hit the ground, which was not unlike an aeroplane during take-off and landing.

The roar of the river alongside echoed a ghostly drone. To have the privilege of visiting this mill with its medieval heritage, and having the opportunity to purchase it was of huge interest and the town hall wanted to declare it as an asset of local relevance since it was deserving of protection. However, as predicted, we were off to a bad start when we found someone jimmying a lock to one of the buildings on the upper level. '*Oh, hello. My father will be with you soon, he cannot find the key so asked me to get the door open.*' At least that is what I think he said in Spanish. We watched expectantly, eager for a glimpse, instead, he just hopped onto his moped and left. The door was still locked.

No more than twenty minutes had passed when a grey-haired man on a push bike arrived. We shook hands, introduced ourselves and waited like children at Christmas about to open their presents.

'*Primero…*' said the man. 'First…'

'Odd they've bricked up these ornate windows, don't you think, Mark?' I pointed as the grey-haired man prised the stubborn door open and gestured for us to follow.

Tentatively we stepped forward into the dark abyss. Large clumps of yellow insulation foam caked the wall.

'That's going to be a bitch to remove,' Mark mumbled. The room was so dark, I used the mobile phone to guide us forward as we followed the grey-haired man further inside.

I had never smelt a dead, bloated hippo floating down a river, but I imagined it would smell something not unlike this room. Somehow, it didn't stop us from following. Call it curiosity? But what truly made the stench more horrific was how it came about in the first place. You see, humans by nature are hard-wired instinctively to react to our olfactory organ – our sense of smell, and react we did, dry retching a little more than I did when it came to laundry with Mark's sweaty socks and knickers.

'What is that smell?' Mark asked. I translated.

'*Piel,*' the grey-haired man answered.

'What did he say?' Mark asked whilst holding his nose between his thumb and forefinger.

'Hang on, I want him to explain. It doesn't make sense.'

The grey-haired man continued to explain, claiming it used to be an old tanning factory that had shut down back in 2008. And much to his amusement, he had decided to show us where the fresh skins had been stored – fresh from the abattoir.

'Right, well, we probably wouldn't be using this room anyway…' I nodded. One for the town hall to preserve I think.

'*Cuidado con el perro,*' the grey-haired man cautioned. Careful with the dog.

Mark's colourful expletives were willfully ignored, because what the man really wanted to say was be careful of the dog poop that covered pretty much every square metre of the 4,000m2 construction. *Poor bastard.* And, if this place is anything like the old Medieval Danish town Odense where ancient stables and well preserved brick houses were unearthed with barrels repurposed as latrines, then we had no hope of ever ridding the property of the smell. Time just cannot alleviate all smells, not if those barrels still smelt like poo after 700 years!

By now, well into our story, we were on our third cup of tea and half a bag of digestives. Sheila's face could very well be compared to a bulldog licking a thistle that had been weed on. However, it is amusing to gross out the mother-in-law, and she thought the little bungalow we viewed that was perfectly preserved after fifteen years complete with greasy frying pan and dirty underwear was bad.

'Well we had better go, there's a fiesta in the village,' Mark said as he stood up.

'OK, darlings, let us know how you get on,' Sheila hugged us and escorted us out the front door.

The Dog Shit place

CHAPTER 5

Snails, nails and piggy tails

As we departed from my mother-in-law's house, Mark's spirits had lifted. Five years ago, we were halfway through our rental contract, running a large vehicle restoration business on the coast. However, one gloomy weekend, we both decided to leave that behind and embark on a new adventure in the countryside. It was a decision deemed both brave and foolish at the time.

'And what are *you* going to do if we leave all of this behind?' Mark asked. I looked out of the car window and groaned. The groves at this time of year remained motionless. No wind rustled the leaves nor provided any respite from the heat. I could hear the smugness in Mark's voice. The truth was Mark could turn heads. He illuminated any room he walked into simply because of his eloquence and charm. Some even compared him to Phil Vickery although; I never really saw the resemblance myself. Moreover, I do not know if it is can't cook or won't cook but Mark did neither cook or wanted to.

There is a lot to be said for committing yourself to marriage. If I had known all those years ago that it involved a grumpy old git laughing at himself as he told a joke such as this:

If women are uncomfortable watching you masturbate then:

A. *They're self-conscious and have intimacy issues*
B. *They're frigid*
C. *They should sit elsewhere on the bus*

Then I might have considered staying single. Marriage is like a secret advertisement for masturbation because once you get that ring on your finger, everything changes. Suddenly your old habits of looking in the fridge, sighing to yourself and then going to bed on an empty stomach – because everyone feels slimmer lying down, change to you looking at the bed, sighing, and then going to the fridge, staying up most of the night tucking into a tub of ice-cream watching Rom-Coms, and having discussions about poo. Mark would purse his lips whilst trying not to laugh as he tries impersonating me, *"Oh I don't do blowjobs. I can only fit a grape in my mouth."* Subtlety was never Mark's forte.

'This relationship is very one-sided,' I answered.

'How so?' he frowned.

'As long as you're pleased then that's all that matters.'

'That's not true at all.'

'It is, even when we topsy-turvy and have foot tickles, you're snoring like an ogre that's just feasted. It's rather off-putting. Then I have your sodding cat rubbing his knob on my pillow. It hardly makes for a romantic evening.'

'You leave Daddy cat out of this, he's old, and he's my boy.'

So in answer to what I planned on doing when we move to the countryside, I answered confidently.

'I'm going to write another book.'

Mark erupted with laughter, and my confidence quickly dissipated. He mumbled a few inaudible words in between his cackling. 'What's so funny? I want to take it seriously, and be able to write full time. What do *you* want to do?' I asked.

'I want to fly my RC planes, and ride my bike.'

'Well, why is your dream any different than mine? You never know…' I'd always dreamt of writing books.

'You're absolutely right, darling. We can always dream. Let's just find somewhere first. It would be great to get out of the rat race, I must admit.'

We continued our journey towards town. Today

there was a fiesta – not sure which one because the Spanish celebrated whenever they had a chance. I always say if it had the word *day* in it then they'd make an excuse to celebrate; celebrating near on 900 festivals over the course of the year. Nor would I recommend trying to comprehend the meaning behind Spanish fiestas, because just when you think they couldn't get any wilder, suddenly you learn that in the far left corner of Spain they celebrate Saint Martha *(Santa Marta de Ribarteme festival)* by parading living people around in coffins. It is believed that Saint Martha's brother Lazarus was raised from the dead when Jesus visited their home. It's their way of showing appreciation for having been spared or to ask to be spared from death.

We parked up next to a huge crowd hovering around an 8ft Paella pan and Mark licked his lips. I watched him as he exited the car with an open mouth. Across the road the familiar ruckus from the valley's Cup de Bernia attracted our attention. A bar/restaurant, and one of the pioneers locally known to have vastly contributed to the tourist boom in the area. Forty years on and he is still exhibiting his skill in front of the sun burnt, red-skinned tourists that passed his door. Bewildered tourists stopped in their tracks as the small white-haired owner poured wine from high above his forehead that trickled down either side of his nose into his mouth. With his free hand he rang a large cow bell and the crowd shouted *Arriba, andalé,* but not quite as enthusiastically as Speedy Gonzalez.

I never remember which of the twins does it, maybe both. Sheila says she can tell the difference, claiming to have almost had one of them. *'That's big Juan,'* she would say, the other being little Juan. Moreover, if she had *had* Big Juan, we might just have been part of one of the wealthiest families in the area. *'You don't have to fancy him, Mother, just marry him.'* Mark proclaimed.

'How long is this Paella going to be until it's ready?' Mark asked absentmindedly as we watched the cook throw in a bucket of chopped onion.

'Probably about half an hour,' I answered, 'I'll ask.'

The cook stirred the sizzling onions with a long 5ft spoon, an impressive spectacle, and I asked him how long it was going to be, as well as what type of Paella he was making. After all, everyone has their own interpretation. Traditionally, Valencian Paella is a combination of meat and seafood.

'Perdona, cuánto va a durar la Paella y que es?' Sorry, how long is the Paella going to take and what is it?

'Unos cuarenta y cinco minutos. Es una mixta,' he replied.

'Mark?'

'Yes, darling?'

'He said about forty-five minutes and it's mixed. Do you really think I'm day-dreaming? That I'm the kind of idiot who thinks we can live off air?'

'No, but the reality is if we do move to the countryside, we will need an income. I didn't know Paella had olives in it.'

'Me either,' I took a closer look. 'That's an eyeball in half a rabbit's head,' I confessed. 'And those are snails.'

'Oh gross. Let's go.'

Pig tails and trotters for sale at our local supermarket

Paella

Paella - is a rice dish originally from the Valencian Community. Paella is regarded as one of the community's identifying symbols

1 38cm Paella steel pan
A generous sprinkling of salt
2 tbsp olive oil
1 onion, chopped – I like to use red onion
1 large garlic clove finely diced
1 tbsp tomato puree
1 diced chicken breast
200g diced pork ribs
1 litre chicken stock
250g paella rice or bomba rice
1 tsp hot smoked paprika
1 tbsp Saffron – can use Paella seasoning as an Alternative
1 400g jar of butter beans / green beans
1 tin of chopped tomatoes
Salt and pepper to taste
½ Sliced Red pepper
½ Sliced Green pepper
1 lemon, cut into 4 wedges
Sprig of Rosemary

Method

Heat the pan over a medium heat and add a

generous sprinkling of salt. Followed by the olive oil. Then add the diced meat and cook until nice and brown. Add the onion and garlic. Lightly soften for 5 minutes...

Add the tomato puree, smoked paprika, and stir until meat is coated.

Add chicken stock and simmer for 5 minutes. Season with salt and pepper to taste and add the saffron.

Add the rice by spreading it evenly around the pan making sure it is covered by the stock and simmer for 10 minutes. We don't want to stir the paella after this point as the rice will release its starch and become mushy.

Decorate the top with your <u>batonnet</u> sliced peppers in a clockwise design alternating the colours.

Simmer for 25 minutes.

Test the rice by tasting the outside.

Remove from the heat when cooked and cover with tin foil, allow it to rest for 10 minutes. Decorate with lemon wedges just before serving.

*Batonnet cut – a French culinary term used for a specific type of cut used especially in the preparation of vegetables. The batonnet cut will leave your vegetables looking like French fries roughly ¼ to ½ wide by 3" long.

The secret to great Paella is the Socarrat – the slightly burnt or rather caramelised rice at the bottom of the pan. If you can achieve Socarrat without burning your Paella, you have made the perfect Paella, so get your spoons out and start scraping.

Paella, what a controversial subject! However, one thing is for sure and that is, you would be hard pushed to find a dish more popular in Spain than Paella.

If you're looking for a typical Spanish dish to transport you spiritually to the Mediterranean coast and be a guaranteed showstopper among your guests at a dinner party then make Paella. After all, Paella is a festive dish, to be enjoyed by friends and family. The largest Paella ever recorded fed 110,000 people cooked in Madrid in 2013 by Antonio Galbis for the Guinness World Record with an unbelievable 6 tonnes of rice, 12 ½ tonnes of meat, 13,000 litres of water and 80 chefs in a 69 foot pan with a world record of using just 1 litre of 'Fairy' to clean it. Now that's using the dish washing liquid sparingly.

The word Paella has that romantic tone to it, and I know if I ever put it on the menu I'd have guests cooing in admiration. It's certainly more impressive than pizza. Imagine, turning up for a cozy night in, and instead of knocking on the door with a bunch of roses in one hand and pizza in the other, you would have a paella pan and a bottle of Rioja. You can thank me later.

Having originated in the city of arts and science *(La Ciudad de las Artes y las Ciencias),* Valencia with its avant-garde architectural design is very much in tune with the 21st century. The Palau de les Arts is oval in shape with a neo-futuristic opera house, and is home to the Orchestra of the Valencian Community. Nevertheless, let us talk about the food. Now, traditionally it is said that Valencian paella does contain snails, in addition to other meat such as pork or chicken. Also, it is cooked over an open flame giving it that fire-kissed taste; however, you can also achieve this by adding Paprika and Rosemary. I've never come across a firm set of rules when it comes to Paella, and many rules I had come to learn about I have seen broken countless of times, but one rule stays and that is:

DO NOT STIR THE RICE.

I have omitted any mollusks from all my recipes, even though eating the slimy creatures isn't just for the French as one might think. According to the BBC, humans ate giant land snails as far back as 170,000 years ago; the Smithsonian claiming paleontologists uncovered parts of a shell in a south African cave from large land snails with signs of heat indicating them to be from cooking, leading them to conclude that snails were indeed part of the human diet. They're also an easy-to-eat fatty protein, an important food source and easy for the elderly who are unable to chew their food. *Shoot me now.*

One of my homemade Paellas

CHAPTER 6

Hamtastic

In a marriage or a long-term relationship, certain things become routine, such as sideward glances and snoring. It's also common to ignore topics that women feel are important to discuss.

This morning, Mark had a look of consternation. Concerned, I asked what was troubling him, and he informed me that he was contemplating going for a poo, so nothing had changed there.

'Mark?' I asked.

'I had a dream last night…I'm stressing over repairing vehicles we don't even have in the workshop.'

'Are you listening to me?' I asked as he munched on a slice of bread.

'What?' Mark looked at me in bewilderment.

'This is meant to be the fun part – house hunting.'

'I found another property…'

'But?'

'It's a two and a half hour drive inland.'

'How much are they asking?'

'Seventy-five grand,' Mark flicked his fingers across the mobile screen scanning the pictures.

No more than a few days later we were hurtling down the motorway, as fast as an old Land Rover can go anyway. The temperature gauge started to climb as we initiated our incline in 42 degree centigrade weather.

'Come on, old girl,' Mark said as he coaxed the old car by stroking the dashboard.

After two and a half hours, and bend after bend, we caught sight of *El Tejar* – what burst into view was an old derelict building divided into several units. It sat on a 73,000sqm plot surrounded by unkempt olive trees and mountainous terrain.

'Buenos dias!' shouted Roman. Roman was the estate agent we were meeting. 'Welcome to El Tejar – what do you think?'

'It looks amazing!' Mark replied.

'Well follow me. I show you around.'

We locked up the car and stumbled across the rough driveway. I was so overwhelmed at the expanse of El Tejar that both Mark and I had already started planning where and what we would do with the property.

'This part is where they kept *los toros*, the bulls,' Roman pointed.

'The previous owners kept bulls here, apparently,' I nodded to Mark. 'How much construction are we talking about, Roman?'

'In total, there is 1800 square meters.'

Even though half of it was falling down, we

continued our tour. Most of the construction had suffered subsidence, and the back building was infested with cockroaches, the odd human excrement, dirty toilet paper, graffiti and random pots and pans. Regardless, Mark and I took it all in.

'What's the catch?' I asked Roman.

'Nothing.' That is when we knew he was not telling the truth. Returning to our car, we began our investigation. Mark and I spoke animatedly the entire journey home. As we spoke about the practicalities of living in one of the units without water and electric, the dream of El Tejar became more of a possible nightmare.

'I do rather like the idea of being completely off-grid.' Mark nodded.

'And for that price, we can install solar right away' The Tejar's romantic charm started to disappear, the cons now outweighing the pros. As it happens, the construction was too close to the main road – in Spain that meant the main road could compulsory purchase the property. Of course, they would wait until you had purchased it first, refuse any renovation permits, allow it to become an even further ruin, then compulsory purchase it for pittance.

As the softening sun started to set, Mark and I returned home, and were drinking tea and feeling self-congratulatory regardless of the outcome.

'Even though our situation isn't ideal, we are lucky that the sun shines,' I smiled, trying to lighten the mood.

'True. We are lucky in that respect. Those poor souls in England would be getting up in the dark and going home in the dark. I remember it so well, such short days there.'

'I wouldn't know,' I replied. 'It sounds so foreign.'

'No, you've been here nearly thirty years. I guess you don't really know any differently.'

'Well, soon we'll be sitting in our Spanish villa thinking about this moment like a distant memory. Even if half of it is falling down,' I laughed. 'You'll be flying your planes and I might get to start my book,' I smiled.

'Yeah, well. That will be a long way off,' he shrugged. Mark didn't read books, had no intention of even picking a book up let alone discussing one, and seeing as my masterpiece hadn't yet seen paper, the thought of me writing a book in the Spanish sun seemed somewhat of a joke.

'If we do manage to buy somewhere, you know it will be a complete ruin. With what I've seen, we'll be lucky to have a roof.'

'I know, but I have to have something to look forward to.'

'I definitely want somewhere with lots of land. I couldn't live on a built-up area or an urbanization like my mother. I must admit, it was very beautiful and picturesque where El Tejar was. I didn't see one foreign car, in fact, not really any cars at all. Even at this time of year.'

'I know what's involved. I'm up for the challenge. It does seem rather unaffected by tourism.'

On our way back, we had stopped at a Spanish tapas bar, much to Mark's dismay. Spanish food, although rated as the third best cuisine to eat worldwide with its 100% Iberian acorn-fed pork, cured cheeses, and of course Valencian Paella can be so damned expensive, and I never really understood why. Home cooked recipes passed down from generation to generation using homegrown produce, and rarely do you receive a plate from a local tapas bar with any of the finesse we're used to seeing on TV with our celebrity chefs. Very few typical Spanish dishes appealed to our tastes. No, Spain is rural and rugged and you would be lucky to get a smile with your *huevos rotos*. As rugged as their cuisine is their tapa names: broken eggs, is as the title suggests; fried eggs with a runny yolk served over cured ham and chips or fried potatoes.

It is more than likely what contributed to Spain being so popular with tourists. Humans by nature are gluttons for punishment and in Spain, especially with food; you take it or leave it. It is pointless complaining, because they simply do not care. As American chef Andrew Zimmern once said, "Please be a traveler, not a tourist. Try new things, meet new people and look beyond what is right in front of you. Those are the keys to understanding this amazing world we live in." Just go with the flow.

The Spanish bar was heaving, and both Mark and I ventured inside. The bar as it was with many was scruffy, the floor littered with peanut casings and olive pips. Traditionally it is customary to throw one's waste on the floor. Apparently, it makes it easier for the waiters to clean plates. Some things don't change from the coast, but what you'll find available in terms of Tapas does.

Where we had found ourselves was a very usual run of the mill Spanish bar. Unlike Madrid, there are not many Ham Museums around here; but Ham bars there are, and can be found throughout Spain, if you ask around. As the USA has Starbucks, Spain has Ham Bars. The Ham Museum concept was founded almost half a century ago, and the family business Marcel Muñoz e Hijos SA are proud to now be recognised as having commercialised their brand both in and outside of Spain, and you'll find these in Madrid.

As we would step out of work and grab a coffee on the go, Spanish would gulp beer and snack on a plate of *Jamón; Jamón Serrano* translating to "Ham of the mountains." Or "Ham from the sierra, or mountain range." White-footed hams that come from pigs that were introduced to Spain in the 1950s, and whilst throughout Europe, *Jamón Serrano* is a prize, in Spain it is considered as an everyday ham. The same cannot be said for *Jamón Ibérico,* mind; the black footed hog is the most genetically purebred animal and the closest to wild boar, and these hams can be anywhere upwards of eight times the price of the more generic *Serrano*. Unlike Italian prosciutto, *Jamón* has more flavour, is less salty and has a lower fat content than its Italian counterpart. *Jamón Serrano* is a source of pride, and a part of every Spaniard's daily life, and is a beautiful accompaniment to any refreshment.

In some major food supermarkets, you can find an array of thousands of pounds worth of different types of *Jamóns.* In addition they are often displayed by hanging high and lining the walls, with one or two mounted on special carving stands. This allows anyone to stop by and have a few wafer-thin slices intricately removed by a staff member as an impromptu snack while you are shopping.

If you find yourself being offered a taste of Bellota Ham, do not pass up the opportunity; it is feral and buttery because the pigs have feasted on acorns and hazelnuts. These hams are exquisite, highly sought after, and are one of the most expensive meats in Europe. They say tastes change, and part of us adapting to a more rural way of life is trying more. We've both never been fans of cured meat made for charcuterie, but a friend recommended us to try *chorizo a la barbacoa*, and it has become our new go-to BBQ meat. With the arrival of paprika from America in the 7th century, the chorizo is distinguished by its reddish colour and whose smoky flavour is brought out when barbecued.

Spanish people are loud; they are full of passion, they enjoy the outdoor life, eating on terraces, and are always socialising with friends and family. Whilst we would find the difference in decibels quite jarring, it is just their way of communicating so don't be alarmed if your hair is blown back with the sound waves if you ever chat to a Spaniard.

The volume indicated just how packed the bar was, and the barista pointed to a single table where we could sit.

'Some things don't change, even when you venture further out from the coast.' I rolled my eyes. The bar was like an old cafeteria, and a long row of men sat at the bar in front of a tapas display. If you're up for trying new flavours then traditional Spanish tapas is a start. Typically, buying a drink in Spain would warrant a free tapa, albeit the portion much smaller than on a tapa menu. If you truly want to integrate with the Spanish, and add it to your bucket list, you will need to *tapear* (going for tapas) at least once.

You would usually find *Gambas al ajillo* Garlic Prawns, *croquetas* the Spanish version of croquettes filled with béchamel sauce, white bread, eggs and any other main ingredient of choice such as Jamón Serrano.

Every single part of an animal is consumed in Spain, and although you won't find it everywhere in the Valencian community, as it originated in

Cordoba, bull's tail stew is a popular dish. *Rabo de toro*, is usually created, and served after bullfights towards the end of summer, and typically found in restaurants near bullrings. The tail is braised, and cooked with onions, red wine, garlic, peppers as well as a variety of herbs and spices.

However, the tail is one of Spain's tamest ingredients. Spain, in general takes food seriously, and dishes traditional to Valencia include many ingredients that neither you nor I would even consider eating. It is to be said that due to the war, the reign of General Franco and overall poverty, the Spanish learnt how to use what was available, and those traditions still carry forth through generations and good home cooking. It originated with the notion of keeping their families fed, but nowadays these recipes are preserved as traditional delicacies. There are no hairs or graces when it comes to these delicacies, in saying that, you will find hair on your deep fried pig's ear if you dared to order *Oreja a la plancha.* Spanish will eat trotters, tails, snouts, testicles, every part of the animal without loss of face. Often the food is just deep fried pieces of pork nose and mouth known as *Morro de Cerdo* that has previously been marinated in a laurel leaf, pepper, garlic and various spices. It is not for everyone, and people either love it or hate it. I've never seen such items on a Tapa menu on the coast, and that's probably because there's no call for it.

However, if you are visiting Spain and the sun

shines, you will soon be trying Aqua de Valencia or at least you should; whilst a closely guarded secret in some places, the amounts in this Valencian cocktail vary, and you will be able to order it in most bars in the city. Made from Cava or Champagne, orange juice, vodka or gin; it should be served in pitchers and drank from a broad cocktail glass.

Nevertheless, Mark and I were not here to sample the variety of Tapas. We both happened to be big fans of Russian Salad *Ensaladilla Rusa*, typically ordering it when we stop at any bar. I didn't realise until recently that it's also known as Olivier Salad, and as the name denotes, a traditional salad dish in Russian cuisine, even though it was supposedly invented by a Belgian cook, Lucien Olivier. The origins of this simple snack vary, one such claim is that the dish in Spain first appeared in a French cookbook in 1856, originally having high-end ingredients such as grouse, partridge, crab, possibly caviar, beef tongue and truffle, but later these ingredients were changed to canned tuna because of the civil war.

So why is it so prevalent in Spanish tapa bars? After all, it's a dish consisting of diced boiled potatoes, green peas, carrots, tuna, mayonnaise and sometimes mustard to enhance the flavour, and now, this simple salad has become one of Spain's legendary meals with every Spanish cookbook having their own version of the recipe. At the end of the civil war even the mention of the word Russian was absolutely prohibited, and the dish was renamed *Ensaladilla National* (the national salad). The dish remains. The name has changed back to Russian Salad. Made and kept chilled, your body will crave this fresh and light snack to combat the heat, served with crunchy small breadsticks called *picos,* it's one of our favourites.

Ensaladilla Rusa

One of the most well-known Spanish tapa dishes.

2-3 medium-sized potatoes
2 boiled eggs
2 boiled carrots
200g of cooked peas
5 gherkins
½ finely diced onion (optional)
Green canned olives sliced in half for decoration
1 tin of canned tuna
Salt and pepper
1 tbsp lemon juice
2 heaped tbsp mayonnaise
Small dry breadsticks (Picos)

Method

Peel the potatoes and carrots and until soft but not mushy, add the peas. Simmer for 2 minutes and rest aside.
Boil the eggs until hard-boiled.
While the eggs are boiling, finely cube the potatoes and carrots. Add, with the peas to a large mixing bowl.
Add finely diced 1 hard-boiled egg, finely diced gherkins and onion (if you're adding it.) Crumble the tuna and gently stir with a wooden spoon.
Season to taste with salt and pepper.

Add mayonnaise a spoonful at a time. You cannot remove mayonnaise so be careful not to add too much. Mix everything thoroughly. You're looking for a coated mixture with the vegetables still visible.

Squirt a dash of lemon – the amount is completely arbitrary depending on how tart you want it.

Spoon into a serving dish and decorate with grated egg and sliced olives.

Chill in the fridge at least two hours before serving.

Serve as a small tapa with a couple of breadsticks.

Patata Bravas

Patata Bravas- are spicy potatoes. A dish native to Spain. White potato cut into 2 cm cubes and pan fried in oil. Commonly served in bars and restaurants throughout Spain as a tapa.

1 kg of good quality white potatoes
3 tbsp olive oil for frying
For the sauce
1 clove of crushed garlic
2 tsp sweet paprika
1 tsp hot paprika
1 tbsp flour
1 tbsp olive oil
1 tsp tomato paste
1 cup of broth

There are two main ingredients in making Patata Bravas – the potatoes and the sauce. The only thing that sets them apart from our familiar chip is the shape. Cut into bite sized squares, they're drizzled in a bright red, spicy sauce. Often accompanied by alioli – a garlic mayonnaise to cut the spice.

Method

Peel the potatoes, rinse thoroughly, and dry with a paper towel.

Cut the potatoes into bite-sized squares.

Heat the olive oil in a large frying pan over a medium heat.

Add the potatoes and adjust the heat to the lowest setting, allowing them to pre-cook for a few minutes without burning.

Remove the potatoes from the heat and allow them to cool. Turn the heat back up to high and add the potatoes back into the pan.

Fry until crispy golden.

Pour the potatoes onto a paper towel to soak up the excess oil.

Sprinkle with salt and pepper.

Mix the garlic, paprika, flour, 1 tbsp olive oil, tomato paste and the broth together in a saucepan and simmer until thickened.

Serve the potatoes with the brava sauce to the side or on top.

CHAPTER 7

Slum bnb and Kevin the pig

Less than a month later, Mark and I found ourselves embarking on the grueling two-and-a-half hour journey once again. This time, we were travelling in our faithful Land Rover to view another property in the Valencian countryside that borders with Albacete.

I had never really considered moving outside of the Valencian province, and I never really had the need to do so either. The average life expectancy for Valencians is 83 ½ years, apparently the healthiest city in the world to live in, and readily accessible to health care. But as Spain's fourth most populous autonomous community with five million inhabitants and a surface area of 23,255.43 km2 there were plenty of places to choose from without moving into another community, and bordering with Albacete meant we were pretty much central to both airports.

Mark slowed the car down so we could take in the view – a flat landscape reminiscent of France.

All of our senses became engaged. On one side of the road, we had green, vibrant vineyards and on the other flat, fields of wheat. Further along we came across olive groves with hundreds of trees and breathtaking views. The mix of smells assaulted our olfactory receptors; a combination of pig manure and floral scents, but it brought smiles to our faces that stretched from ear to ear. We passed through villages whose signage of Welcome and Now leaving were only about 50 yards apart, having a total of 4 inhabitants, and whose narrow streets were lined with artisanal shops selling produce that garnered the tiny village notable.

Without warning, the Land Rover dived off tarmac onto a dirt track. Peering ahead, the old farm building stood alone and majestic surrounded by flat acres of land, and we found ourselves breathless. After parking up, the owners shortly joined us; a Spanish couple that didn't speak a word of English. On the outskirts of this village, we discovered that should we purchase it we would actually become inhabitants 3 and 4.

'Do you hear that?' I asked Mark.

'Hear what?'

'Exactly, it's so quiet.' The stillness was slightly unnerving. The only sign of life as far as the eye could see were a couple of persistent flies. The Spanish couple smiled and took us around the property. It was an old pig farm – empty for the last fifteen years and apart from the odd fresh goat turd, it had remained untouched.

'If it has been empty for fifteen years, why are there fresh goat droppings?' I asked in Spanish.

The old woman laughed, and Mark and I looked

at each other expectantly.

'My cousin was here earlier in the week, they brought a goat,' she replied.

'Uhah…..and?' but she just smiled. The couple stood proud, not really wanting to sell the family business. Raised and sold the pigs to the entire village – she claimed, until her father died. That explained the public abattoir up the road.

'If we're going to buy an old pig farm, Mark, then we definitely need to get a little pig,' I beamed.

'No reason why not, we could be called The Hog House, and those outside pens could be slum bnbs for bikers.' Mark was serious.

Standing in the long corridor, Mark and I looked around, again assessing the 500sqm space.

'He would be called Kevin,' I let my mind drift.

'Why not just go all out and have him called Chris P. Bacon?'

'That's too obvious.'

The Spanish couple just smiled, unlikely they understood a word we were saying.

'Well at least this place has a roof, doors and windows,' Mark whispered. The old Spanish woman had more to show.

'La piscina,' *the pool,* she pointed. *Really?* The building was going cheap, but a pool it didn't have. What was their version of a pool was a concrete hole in the ground. It was amusing how the agent had photo-shopped the water of what could be. There was nothing about the property that hadn't been neglected, but I found myself being charmed by its possibilities nonetheless.

We learnt a lot that day – that despite the property being for sale, it didn't stop the Spanish couple from still emptying the contents of their shopping bags on the sofas inside the adjacent garage that they had set up as a weekend getaway. They pulled out the small camping stove and offered us a drink. It seemed evident that they didn't really want to sell. The old pig farm had been in the family for generations after all, and like a lot of properties, there always seemed to be a disgruntled family member that had grandiose ideas of owning it themselves.

The Pig Farm

CHAPTER 8

There is no love sincerer than the love of food

Mark and I endeavored to keep our composure.

Our dear friends Philip and Winnie, who hailed from Hong Kong, had graciously invited us round for dinner. Both of them were phenomenal cooks, capable in my humble opinion of preparing dishes that would rival those served in a five star restaurant. This gathering was the highlight of our week, and it was impossible to find fault with either of their culinary talents. Philip, in particular, had a playful and debonair demeanor reminiscent of the Galloping Gourmet. With every flip of his spatula and stir of his spoon, he would offer a wink and a smile. Although, Philip didn't wear double-breasted suits like the Galloping Gourmet while he cooked, he did however, always appear with a drink in his hand - a glass of red wine that became an integral part of the show just as much as the food and presentation.

'What's on the menu?' I beamed as we walked through the front door.

'Prawn toast – your favourite…and fish pie. We also got you a gift,' Philip smiled.

'Oh…'

'For when you get your new place,' Philip slid

across a wrapped gift. I opened it eagerly as the two of them busied themselves serving dinner. I unwrapped a book:

All my fucking recipes

'You can write all the recipes you want to cook in this book,' Philip smiled.

'I love it. Thank you.' I was taken aback. I have always had a keen interest in cooking. I remember as a little girl spending time in Germany with my grandparents, and my grandmother would tell me how the Italians taught her how to cook *proper* Italian food. I don't know if that was true but she'd whip up a wicked Carbonara. I still cook pasta to this very day, and I've found property hunting has reignited my passion for cooking. The thought of having my own kitchen excited me, and perhaps one day I too, would have a silly sign hanging up in my kitchen like Phil Vickery that said "What if the Hokey Cokey really IS what it's all about". I was touched that Philip and his wife had gifted me my own *fucking recipe book*, had taken note of my hopes and dreams, and had listened to my many rambles.

It still baffles me that after nearly thirty years and all the different dishes and cultural influences I've had, I have never cooked Paella, or any other Spanish cuisine for that matter. That's going to have to change.

'How did you get on with the pig farm?' Winnie asked.

'I don't think they wanted to sell. We even offered them more money,' Mark shrugged.

'That's Spanish for you. They reel you in, and then leave you disappointed. You'll both get there. You know it's about 3-4 degrees warmer out that way,' Winnie stated.

'And 3-4 degrees colder in the winter, too,' I replied.

'I've even seen a difference of 10 degrees, but I love the seasons. One thing I miss from England; spring, autumn, I'd love to go back to that weather climate with a little more sunshine though,' Mark interjected.

That beautiful balmy evening, the four of us sat outside near the pool watching the sunset behind the skyline of the sea. Philip and Winnie's home sitting high among a nest of equally beautiful homes – apart from one neighbour with purple hair who enjoyed parading around in the nude, holding wild parties, serving marihuana cocktails and promoting a healthy vegan lifestyle. Money can't buy taste, but it can buy the freedom to not give a toss.

'Reminds me of Hong Kong that view does,' Philip said as he ignored his neighbour's shenanigans. 'Bloody lunatics next door, do you know what the latest is?'

'No, tell us,' I asked, now intrigued.

'Fuckers reported me to the *Guardia.* They said I

was being a pervert.'

'What?' Mark laughed.

'Might laugh now, but Spain takes things like that very seriously,' I said as I kicked Mark's shin.

'Because they caught me looking as I was getting the bike out.'

'Why were you looking?' I raised my brow.

'I wasn't *looking*… I was backing the bike out of the garage and she was just standing there with her baps out and a hosepipe in her hand, watering the garden.' Philip swigged another mouthful of wine and turned up the music's volume, intentionally to annoy his neighbours.

'Any more drinks?' Winnie asked.

'Yes, please'

'Please,' Mark and I answered.

Admittedly, their home was beautiful. The piece de resistance was the outside glass room, kitted out with stainless steel kitchen appliances, large oak dining table and chairs, and state-of-the-art BBQ smoker and grill. The smoky, mouth-watering smell of the sizzling BBQ of a previous dinner was nostalgic of better times for Mark and I. Philip had this machine down to a T, but the last time I used a BBQ it was gas and I singed a few facial hairs so since then Mark has taken the role of chief Barbecue cook even though it had been some years before we had enjoyed such outdoor living.

Although the sea offered that blue-velvet paradise where seagulls and their raucous caws would dive, floundering in and out of the blue waters provided light entertainment, and the pelagic tangy aroma of salt and seaweed wafted through your home, and enveloped your clothing making you feel like you're always on holiday, both Mark and I had made up our minds.

'I've lived on coastal Spain for a long time, I'm fed up. We both are. Neither of us are real beach-goers. I don't think we have been down to the beach more times than you can count on one hand.'

Mark rubbed my arm in an unusually sympathetic way.

'It's true. The sea is too salty for my taste. You know they've brought in a new law saying you're not allowed to piss in the sea…like anyone is going to see…'

'Crazy seeing as they've closed the beach several times this year because of sewage,' Philip laughed.

'Another reason why we don't swim in the sea,' I scoffed.

'Our dream awaits, Abs. We'll get there. Good things come to those who wait,' Mark suspired.

'It's all taking a toll. I have a doozy of a spot on my chin,' I sulked.

'I know,' Mark acknowledged.

'You've seen it?' I asked.

'Hard not to, it's like a ferking, red traffic light,' he shrugged.

Winnie scoffed her wine. 'You two should have a reality TV show.'

'Like Love Island?' I crinkled my forehead.

'No, like Escape to the Chateau…' Philip toasted.

'More like Escape to the Shiteau,' I laughed.

Outside living – a room with a view

CHAPTER 9

Cosmic ordering or just positive thinking?

'Señora, por favor,' the salesperson on the end of the phone pleaded in a male, east-Asian accent.

'Oh, piss off!' I yelled as I hung up the receiver.

'Another call from Microsoft?' Mark asked.

'Yes. And since when did I become a Señora, not a Señorita?'

'Since you started hanging around me,' Mark laughed.

The word Señorita in Spain typically referred to young and or single women. It seemed odd to me that in Spain people would assume you were married or widowed and addressed you as such.

It was not long before we were again spending our free time looking for yet another property. Once again, Mark and I started browsing the internet for land, and a property big enough to keep people away. Somewhere wooded, quiet and preferably flat sounded idyllic. Historically, most of Spain's population resides on the coast, and many towns and cities have developed along the coastline because the sea has been a source of not only food but transportation. We also discovered whilst house-hunting that the coast has a much milder climate, which for settlers has made it more appealing. The country is one of the most climatically diverse places in the world, and being dominated by five major climate regions means greater heat waves and drier weather with increasing climate change. Mark and I started looking at properties in the height of August, and saw a huge difference between inland areas with having a greater seasonal difference than the coast; the countryside or *campo* having usually hotter temperatures than the coast regularly exceeding 35 degrees Celsius. We have experienced a difference of 8 degrees in July. By contrast, the campo winters easily drop up to -10 degrees Celsius. In addition, the higher above sea level you go, the colder it gets. Rarely would you need a log-burning stove, see snow or experience seasonal changes if you lived on the coast, and that was something we missed.

With our inland adventures, I had never seen windmills so prolific before, and even though we were outside what is now considered modern Spain, I couldn't help but wonder what these white, gargantuan, forestall statues had to offer the peace and serenity of authentic, traditional Spain. I have certainly seen a fair share of change in the years I have lived here, but one thing that doesn't change is the food. Sure, if you visit Barcelona or Madrid you'll find your liquid nitrogen vanilla ice cream, passion fruit caviar, dehydrated cranberry and blueberry with flower petal confetti. Foams and aromatic smoke to surprise you and have you taste with your eyes and what not. But this won't give you an ounce of information on traditional Spanish cuisine or their culture. If you do find yourself visiting Albacete, however, try Café Bar El Filo de La Navaja – it is run by a family who opened their doors over 50 years ago; breaded cod being a specialty of the house since 1968. It's not going to knock your socks off, but it is good, wholesome, home-cooked Spanish food. If you want to see Spain as it was thirty years ago, then I highly recommend taking a trip to Alcalá del Júcar (in the province of Albacete) – a magical village that has been a historical site since 1982, and sits on a steep hill overlooking the Júcar river. *Stunning.* Some would argue its one of the most picturesque villages in Albacete and even in Spain. Its dramatic gorge will take your breath away: A true hidden gem. By boarding the boat in the Roman town of Cofrentes you'll experience the breath-taking landscape of canyons and rugged mountains towering 400 meters above you with a relaxing river cruise along the Jucar river.

In Alcalá del Júcar, dominating the hill you'll find a medieval Arab fortress with panoramic views, so be sure to take your camera, and don't forget the restaurant/nightclub combo Devil's Cave, the tunnel runs from one hill across the other – grab a beer and enter one end and exit the other.

Mark and I had made up our minds. Moving inland not only appealed more to our budget, but also the way of life. Our prayers were answered with this other property. Our good friend Lydia had drummed it into me that if we really wanted something we were better off cosmic ordering it, so I did as she suggested.

1. Must have outbuildings

2. I'd like grass – Mark said - Although a tall order in Spain.

3. The pink almond blossom is beautiful, wouldn't it be grand if we had one of those in the garden!

4. Chickens – we've got to get chickens.

5. Outside dining. Life in Spain is spent outside. 'I want to BBQ. BBQ all the time, and not gas, I want proper charcoal.' Mark laughed.

The list went on and on, and we enjoyed throwing ideas back and forth of things we wanted from a property. A little adventurous for the pittance we had to offer, but it was nice to dream.

A childhood memory before I moved to Spain was living in the country in the south of England. My family lived not too far from pig farms, all bound by fields and the rolling hills of West Sussex. Even though I was knee high to a grasshopper, I still remember the tiny hamlets, and places like Arundel Castle just takes my breath away even today. I guess those early memories of that quintessential region of England that for me, feels like a work of fiction, a place so beautiful and charming it could really only be found in a storybook. Clearly and firmly embedded in the back of my mind, and I found myself nearly thirty years later looking for that very thing. However, finding flat land, especially grass, seemed near impossible living on the Spanish coast. Nevertheless, looking for property with a not so large budget makes you realise that there is more to Spain than the sea. Living on the Spanish coast was all I had ever known in terms of Spain, and the distant rapidly fading memories of the UK. As foreigners, we all have this preconceived notion of what Spain is, but the truth is the country is so vast, with so much to offer that unless you go out and explore it, you will never know, and you might find a bargain or two.

The beautiful river cruise along to Jucar river

CHAPTER 10

The Deed was done

Low and behold this property ticked the boxes - well most of them, and Mark and I found ourselves the proud owners of a country home. The enchanting property had us falling in love as soon as we saw it. It far exceeded anything in our wildest hopes and dreams – everything else that we had been looking at rarely had a roof let alone doors and windows.

Having looked far and wide, we knew we wanted a restoration project, a home we could make our own, and large enough that Mark and I wouldn't kill each other.

However, not only did it have doors and windows, it had a brand new charcoal BBQ and two bags of charcoal. *It was fate*. Amazingly it also had among the some three hundred olive trees, three almond trees – not in the middle of the garden but then I didn't specify where I wanted them did I? There was also a small patch of grass growing fervently between the house and the garage so Mark was happy, and there was more…

It had taken us five years before this dilapidated farmhouse surrounded by hundreds of olive trees charmed us, despite the hideous interior décor consisting of 1960s yellow polypropylene furniture, and a 1970s cabinet that fell apart as I opened the door to look inside.

Although a tremendous project to behold, the overall impression was calm. It sat at the foot of two mountainsides and was bordered by more olive groves. With little over 3 ½ acres, it was just what we were looking for. 'It's so quiet, I feel like I'm going to be sat around a campfire playing the banjo,' Mark said in wonderment.

We questioned each other's sanity, in whether we were making the right decision to move, but the pull was far too great. *Where there is a will there is a way.* Could we be self-sufficient to a degree living on a small farm? Could we be homesteaders? Why not! Anyone can farm, if you have ever grown a tomato plant, then you have farmed. I had already started planning vegetable gardens, and we were definitely planning to get chickens. So, after nearly three decades of that haunting childhood memory, I found myself full circle once again living in the countryside, and wanting a little piglet of our own.

That hot day in August we stepped through the yellow, dry stalks of the front garden. Each one stabbing at the side of my leg as we took in the vast property. And like Van Gogh and his painting *View from the Wheat Fields*, I was amazed at the intense colour that could only be described as oil painting as the dry, yellow grass shimmered under the golden sun. How many properties had the countryside at the foot of the front door? Objectively I could say it was truly beautiful. However, the dry grass was not the only thing moving among our feet. Without warning, thousands of grasshoppers leapt into the air.

Mark's hand entwined with my own, and we gawped. Never had we seen an invasion quite so prolific. I had heard of the grasshopper plague of 1874 following the Civil War where during the heat of a particularly hot summer, the drought was not the most devastating thing to occur for farmers. Insects arrived in swarms consisting of millions of flying insects that blocked out the sun and sounded like hail. They demolished crops as well as stripping wool from the backs of living sheep. More recently aired a documentary leaving viewers sleepless as they filmed a super-swarm that spanned across 200 square miles claiming that generally locusts tend to be solitary animals. The young hoppers taking around four weeks to become adults unless they have optimal conditions, then their maturity fast-tracks, with each locust consuming their bodyweight in vegetation per day, swarms can destroy tonnes of vegetation, each swarm joining another as they move in search of food; forming gigantic plagues several billion in size and as big as forty miles wide.

As we walked around the property, and viewed the existing ruin that formed part of the farm, we were dumbfounded as to why there were several animals still there: two dogs, around twenty hens, partridges and pigeons…

'They'll be gone soon, not to worry,' we were assured by the agent. Of course, we peeked through the wire fence and spoke to the chickens, waving our fingers to stroke their combs and wattles. Grasshoppers escaped our footsteps by plunging into the pen of doom, and the chickens gave us light entertainment by running after them, devouring several within a few seconds.

That solves our plague issue, we're definitely getting chickens.

The entrance led to a metal and glass door that opened up onto a large, wide enclosed *naya,* a once outside covered terrace that had now been enclosed; a rarity in Spanish houses. As we ventured further inside, we were taken into a central room with a large obtrusive fireplace. A bathroom and storeroom were to the right, a downstairs bedroom straight ahead alongside a staircase and kitchen.

I pursed my lips as I wandered round. The smell of damp and dust indicating the home had been shut up for some time. Fly carcasses scattered along the skirting and inside the stone fireplace. An old sofa that had seen better days looked uninviting, and Mark sat in a red, tired leather chair sinking to the floor. 'OH', he laughed as the springs let loose. Straight away I could imagine myself cooking up a storm in the kitchen that to our surprise looked fairly new, and would certainly see us through for a good year. The whole house inside and out had had a fresh coat of white paint, yet both Mark and I had tried to avoid such boring, neutral tones for fear of it looking too sterile, but it offered a wonderful blank canvas for us to add some textures and vibrant touches here and there.

The stairs were central to the dining room and led up to a further three bedrooms, with beautiful views across the valley and our garden.

We learnt a bit that day and the subsequent months since we first saw *the house*; that there really did exist bold, daring eagles that would swoop down and snatch a pigeon mid-flight without any hesitation or fear of your presence. Everyone has solar panels even though electricity pylons aren't that far away, and the village mayor is your man and the only man who delivers water in a 5000 litre water tank on the back of his tractor.

Getting Christmas out of the way meant we could sell up our business and move in to the property in February, and we discovered that our presence to this small village was more newsworthy than actual news because you know, in a small village everyone becomes a top-level reporter. And if there is a local fiesta, then there really was nowhere to buy groceries so it would be wise to be growing our own. However, all jokes aside, Spanish village life has its appeals. If you can integrate and connect with the locals, they'll go above and beyond to help you should you need it.

We just had one problem. The original owner didn't want to leave.

CHAPTER 11

The burning of the giant polystyrene

That February will be a month etched into our memories. A month we will never forget. With just four weeks to complete work, pack and move to the house, Mark had the unfortunate accident of falling off a ladder and broke his leg. If I were to describe this old goat in one word, it would be stubborn; he had seventeen staples and broke three casts.

We moved in with a five-car convoy during the peak of the Fallas festival, a Spanish tradition celebrated in and around Valencia to honour Saint Joseph. The event is a unique blend of satire, art and lunacy that should not be missed. The festivities include a pyrotechnic firework display that lights up the night sky for miles. Locals spend weeks creating ephemeral art sculptures of a satirical nature, often with deep religious roots, ranging from three to twenty meters in height. They can depict both fantasy and real-life scenes.

According to Mark's new friend Juan, whom he met through the Radio Control flying club we discovered, Juan is also a falla creator on a small scale. He shared that the tradition originated from way back from the Valencian people's custom of piling up leftover wood in front of their houses and eventually burning it come spring.

Slowly these random piles of rubbish began taking shape, becoming more humorous, even criticising public figures, and so in medieval Valencian language, the act became Fallas. With the help of carpenters and painters, each display was made from wood, wax and clothing, cardboard soon becoming a popular medium and replaced wax as the main material. From the 1970s, the fallas figurines became polystyrene. Falla artists began emerging as they gained in complexity and size, each artist owning their workshops as they invent their own unique styles costing well over €100,000 each, the most expensive being that in 2009 one went for a million euro. *Then they burn them.*

If you think setting fires in what was then a walled city is crazy, then you haven't been to Spain. Because what country would one minute say you couldn't drive a car in a city unless it was the new low emission engine, and then burn tonnes and tonnes of polystyrene?

There are many occurrences and traditions in Spain I'll never be able to comprehend, and it hurts my head to try to do so.

And where the money comes from is anyone's guess. Queen of the falla festival is called a Fallera Mayor. This is where you'll see a girl over the age of 15 being chosen as a representative based on the criteria: Communication skills, speech, responsibility, her knowledge of the local culture and so on. It's a long and complicated selection process but also one of great honour and she'll be expected to contribute financially to the falla principal. Her dress made from silk will be in the region of €1000 to even over €10,000, the dearest dresses being made to order from hand-woven silk.

Mark feeling sorry for himself

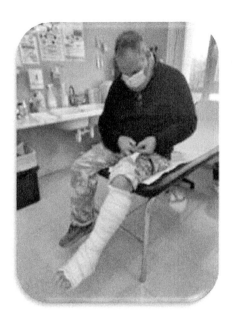

Spanish Tortilla
(Potato Omelette)

Tortilla Española is a traditional dish celebrated as an essential part of Spanish cuisine. You'll find it in most Spanish bars as part of the tapa menu.
The Spanish tortilla is made with thinly sliced potatoes, onions, eggs and slowly cooked in olive oil. It derives much of its taste from the olive oil so do invest in a good quality extra virgin olive oil..
This wonderful vegetarian tapa dish will surely impress your dinner guests and it's so easy to make.

2 medium potatoes peeled and cut into quarters
8 fresh room temperature eggs
Olive oil for frying
Salt and pepper
1 onion finely diced (optional)

1 x Sarten de tortilla (I have found the double frying pan special for tortillas a life-saver, and you can buy them off Amazon for a great price.) Alternatively a standard non-stick frying pan and a plate will do.

The trick with tortilla is to cook on a low heat

Method

Wash and peel your potatoes and cut them into quarters, add them to a pot of water. Boil until soft but not fluffy.

Adding onion is entirely arbitrary, but it's a must for me. Fry your diced onion in olive oil on a low heat until softened. Meanwhile, beat your eight eggs in a large mixing bowl. Add salt and pepper.

Drain the boiled potatoes and cut into small 1cm cubes, set aside to cool. Once cool, add to the eggs.

Set onions aside to cool, and then add to the egg mixture.

In the same frying pan as your onions, pour in your egg and potato mixture, gently move to remove air and fry for 15 minutes on a low heat. If using the special tortilla pan, flip and fry until golden brown.

Rest tortilla and serve cold with a dollop of mayonnaise if you wish.

Traditionally the tortilla is flipped using a plate, however you can place the pan under the grill which will finish cooking the top.

I have always cooked Tortilla with onion and will likely always do so. It's not to everyone's taste, and the tortilla can be cooked just as well without it. But from those that have asked me for the recipe I recommend the sweetness the onion adds, especially if you use sweet or red onion.

* How rare you prefer your tortilla is down to personal choice. Some leave almost no curd, whilst some are quite runny. Try both.

CHAPTER 12

"Never wrestle with pigs, you both get dirty and the pig likes it." George Bernard Shaw

Fortunately, Mark is a useful handyman. Duncan calls him a c**t in the nicest possible way, because there doesn't seem to be anything Mark cannot do. *"He even cuts trees down in a straight line, c**t."* But when there is so much to do, where do you start?

We were yet to buy ourselves a bed, so for now, we slept on a mattress. After moving out of the downstairs bedroom due to dampness, we ended up waking up in the middle of our conservatory. It was 2:00 am, and the old farmer's dog, which he had tied up to a tree, was barking relentlessly.

'What is he barking at?' I asked as I rolled out onto the floor.

'I don't know. I can't see a thing. I'm going to go check it out.' Mark replied. He opened the front door and stepped outside slowly and quietly, trying not to make any noise as he approached the dog. It wasn't one of his wisest moments; we were in the middle of nowhere. Curiosity got the better of me, so I decided to follow him. Suddenly, the dog stopped barking, and we heard a rustle, the breaking of twigs, and the occasional grunt. We stopped dead in our tracks, wide-eyed and desperately looking around.

'Probably just the little one,' Mark assured me, referring to the farmer's other dog who roamed freely. Nevertheless, I walked closer to him. If there was anything out there, I figured I could outrun him and hightail back to the safety of our door.

'Did you grab the torch?' he asked.

'I did…'

'Well, put it on then…' At his wish, I shone the torch; a large angry hog with three piglets stood next to the dog, and they stared directly at us.

'Don't move…' Mark suggested, but I was already running back to the door.

It didn't really resemble any pig we'd seen before. A massive thick-set body on thin short legs, arched back stiff with bristly hairs, and large tusks protruded from its lower jaw. And when it squealed, it figuratively made us shit our pants.

'RUN!' Mark yelled as he ran for safety towards me, holding the door open. Behind the safety of our door, we shone our torch, and the pigs continued their forage ignoring the dog chained to the tree.

We gazed out of the glass door, observing and listening to the foraging swine, and were left pondering the dog's chances of survival through the night. We captured photographs; the pigs were visibly startled by our presence but remained completely unfazed, as if they were oblivious to our existence. With no natural predators, these hogs had little to fear.

Mark sighed, 'I think my sphincter blew a kiss.'

'You're fortunate that's all it did. If we had been any closer, we both might have required a change of underwear.' I acknowledged. Furthermore, given this sow had offspring, our odds of becoming hamburger meat were ever so slightly higher.

The dog's survival was a relief. I suspected it was not the first time he encountered such company. We contemplated showing the farmer the photographs we had taken, but given our knowledge of him, he and his posse would likely arrive with great enthusiasm and turn up all gung-ho.

We managed to get a couple of hours of sleep, interrupted by waking up to tell the dog to be quiet. However, this arrangement was far from satisfactory. We could not continue on like this.

The next morning the sun shone through the glass onto our quilt. Mark started a fire in our log burner, and we enjoyed a cup of tea like a pair of teenage campers. The sun had barely risen over the mountainside when we took our cups outside to watch the sunrise.

Suddenly, we were startled by the sound of a cat's cry. At that time, we were unaware of the wide variety of bird species in the area. On the coast, you would be lucky to spot a vulture in the distance as it circled its next meal. Spain is home to over four hundred bird species, accounting for approximately 60% of all birds in Europe. It is a popular destination for bird enthusiasts. We had never seen such a diverse range of bird species before, so it never occurred to us that this catcall was actually a bird.

Wild boar at the front door

CHAPTER 13

Duncan

Duncan had been the sole respondent to our advertisement for a labourer. It appeared that not many people in this region were eager to work, so we were surprised to hear from a fifty-nine year old British man who had been residing in Spain for almost eight years. He appeared to be diligent and sociable, hardworking and chatty enough, engaging in deep conversations within the first few days. Upon slamming the car door shut, he declared, "Call me Dunc." His name has since become a long-standing joke because he is always looking to dunk it into some unsuspecting woman.

Today was no exception; the temperatures had soared well into the mid 30's. I took a deep breath of hot air. When it gets this hot, it's like holding a hair dryer in front of your face. Mark removed his shirt while we sat outside with a cup of tea, and looked around.

'Not like you to get your tits out in front of Duncan, Mark!' I joked.

'Duncan doesn't mind, do you, Dunc?' Mark shrugged. Duncan had been away in Almeria for the last 10 days. We hadn't heard a word from him, but knowing him as we did, the reason probably involved a woman.

'Mate, I had sex 3 days ago. If I hadn't had that, I'd be over there sucking on those tits.'

'Oh, Jesus,' I laughed.

'Most of the birds on the coast are drinkers or dopers. I've waited two years for this broad, I had to get it out of my system,' Duncan shrugged.

'So, this one on the coast, the one that treated you horribly for the last two years…' Mark began.

'Yes, that one,' Duncan nodded.

'I thought you'd slept with her already?' I asked.

'No. I couldn't get it up. I got it partially of the way in. That's when I found out there was something wrong. *"Not fucking me with no pills,"* she yelled. Anyway, I did it. She just lay there; it was like shagging a dead body anyway.'

'I wouldn't know,' Mark mumbled. 'It's on the to-do list though,' he laughed.

'Well, I mean lifeless. Anyway, that's done and dusted. Not like you have a problem, Mark. You're a good looking chap,' Duncan toasted.

'Don't get him started. When Mark puts on his brown, leather jacket he already thinks he's Jack Reacher.' I tittered.

'Jack Reaching…I don't know where you get these ideas from, Abs.' Mark blurted.

'Dunc, you didn't tell her then that this time you were on the blue pills?' I asked.

'Fuck no.'

'And was it worth the wait?' I asked.

'Nah I put my hand down there and it was like stroking a dog. I hoped she might change…' he sighed.

'Not shaved in a while?' Mark said.

'Nah, I don't think she's had any for years to be honest. I hoped once I'd dicked her she'd change but she's just cold; wouldn't hold my hand or anything,' Duncan hung his head low.

'It sounds like her idea of friends with benefits meant you coming round and doing the gardening,' I stated and Mark agreed by nodding his head.

'Yeah. I know. Anyway, on my way back I got this message off another woman.'

'Oh right?'

'She's Brazilian, looks like a goddess,' Duncan started.

'That's asking for trouble. Got to ask yourself why she's single then,' Mark advised.

'Mind you, although we've video messaged, I've only seen the top half. If she's got an arse like a fucking baboon I'm not interested.'

Duncan had been single for three years, and his ex-girlfriend still visited him to do her laundry, even though she was seeing someone else; the long-haired lover from Liverpool, Duncan called him.

Not long after meeting Duncan, Mark and I organised a Singles night in town. Perhaps there was someone in the area who had yet to meet Duncan.

'What about a nice Spanish lady?' I suggested.

'Yeah, suppose, if she speaks a little English,' he shrugged. 'Just got to be careful around here, too many English all gossiping. That's why I go to the coast, no one knows me there. When I first moved here, I met this person who was selling a house, and it belonged to the brother or sister, they kept saying I had to pop round - but I took a friend with me, you know because I got the impression they were a bit pervy. Friend joked that they were going to tie me up as a gimp and ride me rotten. So, from then on I've always been a bit wary. They are back in Spain now, Swingers, as blatant as they come. You know, when you joke about stuff, you don't really go into too much detail, but he did, so you can tell. I honestly thought he was going to put something in my drink, ball in my mouth and ride me rotten. You never know when you buy a house in the mountain.' Duncan took a deep drag from his cigarette, savoring the last bit of smoke and coughing as he did so. He seemed unsure about how to dispose of the butt, as there was no bin nearby. Reluctant to flick it into our garden, he extinguished it by stubbing it out on the stone bench and carefully returned it to its packet.

'Another tea?' I asked.

'Yeah why not,' Duncan replied. 'So when are you organising the singles night?'

'We can do next Friday if you want?'

'Great.'

The following Friday arrived quickly, and although no one showed up, the three of us had a great time, and Duncan shared more stories with us.

Disheartened, he said, 'I think I'm just going to give up.' Mark shook his head and advised him to stop being so pessimistic, adding that he wouldn't find a lady if he, and I quote, 'just wants to bang her.'

'Oh no, I don't say things like that. I can be quite the gentleman.'

I stood up to get another round of drinks.

'Then what's the problem? You're not a bad looking guy!'

'Even a dwarf wasn't that interested…'

'Pardon me?' Mark spurted.

'I was very young. My mate and I went to a club, he took the tall one, and I hooked up with the shorter one. I didn't realise just how small she was until we danced. I knew it was time to go when she asked me to dance, and her head was at my crotch, but you know, she was a human being that wanted a bit of cock. I did my bit – took her out to the car, bounced her up and down on my lap, banged her and took her home,' Duncan admitted.

'For Christ's sake, Duncan.' I whispered. Mark was in hysterics. There was no stopping the hysteria now, and that's when we first met Yesenia.

'Oh, what about her?' Duncan gestured as he saw a table of raven haired beauties.

I raised my brow and looked to my side, 'She's

looking at me more than you, Dunc. I think she bats for the other side.'

'Typical.'

CHAPTER 14

Hogs r us

'Well, that's it, we've got to be called The Hog House now,' Mark exclaimed.

'It is quite fitting, hogs being Harley Davidsons too, and with our vaulted ceiling, we'll have a medieval tavern, with an old wagon wheel and candles suspended from the ceiling. It will be called The Hog's Head!' I envisioned an old Spanish 17th century oak table playing host to various seasonal gatherings.

'You have a very active imagination. I'll add it to the list of everything else we have to do.'

It would be reminiscent of a bodega we used to frequent for our weekly lotto ticket. Bodega Riko is a stone clad building founded in 1947. It has that old medieval appearance that I love so much, and the brother and sister who run it offer guided tours starting in the field of vines. The tour immerses you into the valley's history of wine making, how the Americas had brought over the fungal blight of Phylloxera that decimated the fields back in the mid 19th century, and you'll be able to walk away with a perfectly drinkable wine for the measly price of around £2 per litre or less.

If it wasn't for our basic bathroom facilities it

would feel like we were living in the Middle Ages. I'd be flapping an *Abanico* (Spanish fan) not to keep cool, or repel insects, but to rid the smell. Thank goodness, four months of the year it was warm enough to bathe without freezing to death. Back in the Middle Ages, they did take baths albeit in a single tub, filled with hot water and shared among many, often the water becoming so dirty it would kill a baby.

Our dining room still boasted wooden beams, which had been concealed by a false ceiling installed by the previous Spanish owners. However, this alteration obscured the beautiful gable roof, and the beams were purely decorative. Fortunately, we didn't encounter any rats or cockroaches when we lifted one of the tiles. Consequently, when heavy rainfall caused the roof to leak, we were spared the sight of these creatures running and scurrying through our home.

We aspired to restore our cortijo in a manner that would benefit the farmhouse. Our vision was to blend both antique and rustic furniture that would complement the property's character. With the region's geography, it made the local flea markets rich with remnants of the Middle Ages, including wagon wheels, armour, antique furniture, and eerie Victorian dolls. Many towns in the area boasted impressive walled castles, grand cathedrals, and monasteries. During our explorations, Mark and I visited Fontilles Leprosarium in Murla. Established in 1902 in the Val de Laguar, this site now stands as a historical testament to the eradication of leprosy – an affliction that plagued Europe during the Medieval period between 1000 and 1400AD. The sanitorium was created with the notion of providing a better quality of life and medication to leper patients in both the Alicante and Valencian region. The hospital was opened in 1909 for not only medical treatment but research and education. In 1924 it became a village with bakers, carpenters, shoemakers, hairdressers and many more facilities. Neighbouring villages protested at the possible escape of patients so a nine-foot tall and two foot thick wall extending two miles was constructed which took seven years to build. It stands to this day and is a prominent feature.

My phone pinged several messages in succession. It was Yesenia wanting to meet up later on, and then finalising her messages in her usual way *Hogs n Snogs.*

Born in Australia to Spanish parents and raised in Canada, she speaks with a Canadian accent. Today, she was complaining that her friend and hairdresser had cut off about a foot of her hair. As black as poet's ink, her soft curls sway like beach grass in the wind, and her smile is contagious. It would go viral faster than a rat up a drainpipe. When you're in the company of Yesenia, you find yourself surrounded by acquaintances who are eager to embrace her positive energy and warmth. It's either that or her ample physical attributes. However, Mark and I discovered that Exaggeration is her middle name. In reality, her hair looked lovely.

'Hey, babe,' Yesenia greeted me with the customary Spanish kiss on both cheeks. A sign of warmth and familiarity that is cherished in Spanish culture. Although I have lived in Spain for a long time, I still tense up as I am British and only show affection to dogs and cats. In reality, this tradition involves merely touching cheeks and making the kissing sound "mwah". However, the Spanish can be known for their lack of personal space, so don't be too alarmed if someone you don't know touches you; they're just being friendly.

'So, babe, where shall we go?' Yesenia said.

'We can't be long. We have an appointment.'

'Oh, what about?' she asked.

'If I told you, I'd have to kill you.'

And so the renovation begins. Old wooden beams were revealed behind the false ceiling.

CHAPTER 15

Just one bullet.

Mark gulped a can of Coca Cola, and stared out of the car window. I could see in his eyes he was, in this very moment, contemplating how we came about the circumstances we found ourselves in, but the truth of the matter was that the reality of the situation was far different than it appeared. I sighed deeply as we waited. It was almost 9 o'clock at night, according to the digital display in the old Land Rover, and the night started to draw to a close. At this time of the year, it didn't get dark until about now, so we hung on so we could venture out under the cloak of darkness before we departed the vehicle. Waiting patiently, we silently observed, careful not to draw any attention to ourselves - two Brits sitting ominously in their car. Time had never stood still for so long nor been so quiet. It was deafening.

We weren't given many instructions, just to be here, today, a Tuesday evening at 9 o'clock. Other than that, we didn't know what to expect. We'd already waited half an hour, not wanting to be late. The saying goes if you're on time then you're already late, and this wasn't someone we wanted to start off on the wrong foot with.

The clouds loomed overhead, casting ominous shadows on the ground below. The distant rumble of thunder signaled the impending arrival of rain. As the first drops began to fall, I quickly wound up my window, bracing myself for the heavy downpour that would soon follow. The sound of raindrops pounding against the aluminium roof of our agricultural vehicle filled the air, as we continued our wait through the stormy weather.

Mark slowly and quietly unlatched his seatbelt, readjusting his position in the car. He hoped that our movements would not attract the attention of any unsuspecting passerby outside the small bar nearby. The bar was integrated into townhouses on either side. Tables were out the front with chairs pulled forward and leaning against them. A bright purple Bougainvillea plant strangled the metal framework in front of the sole window, while a couple of men stood outside puffing on cigarettes. It was a dismal sight, and neither of us was interested in visiting the bar, especially since we didn't drink alcohol.

Yet the gloomy bar appeared to beckon the local patrons and sucked them into its depression. Spanish bars rarely had any atmosphere; bright LED lights like an old school canteen. When the men finished their cigarettes, they squeezed back into the crowded bar. The deafening drone was inescapable. We had heard rumours the bar was *the* place to go, you know, if you *had* to meet someone associated with illegal activities. Everyone just kept their heads down and stayed out of everyone's business – we had come to learn that it was the way in small villages, so that's what we did.

As our eyes watched the crowd, a man over 6ft tall and heavy build caught our attention. He skulked towards the entrance of the bar, hunched over with his hands in pockets. Immediately we sensed that this was probably who we were waiting for. He certainly looked like he was capable of more than mere violence. *"Just don't look at his eyes, he doesn't like that."* we were warned.

'You're having a laugh aren't you?' I replied at the time.

'He usually comes in around 9 o'clock, but I didn't tell you. Got it?' the server had said as she looked side to side over her shoulders.

The man in question was called Pedro, at least, that's the name we were given. That's all we were told – the guy to go to if you wanted something sourced and dispatched. He wasn't the typical suit-wearing type that we're used to seeing in movies, real killers are rarely suave, and I've never known one to wear a suit –not that I've met many killers. This guy was a greasy, pot-bellied Spaniard that you wouldn't want to meet down a dark alley that's for sure. There were plenty like him around and he blended in perfectly.

'Let's get this over and done with, Mark,' I sighed as we exited the car. 'Let me do the talking.'

Mark still didn't speak much Spanish, but with

his olive skin and dark hair, no one would know.

'We don't want you saying *si* and agreeing to something too sinister, all right? From what the waitress told us, this guy has a reputation of being especially brutal, easily lifting a 260lbs corpse over his shoulder,' I reminded him.

'Abbie, when it comes to money, I leave the negotiating up to you.'

CHAPTER 16

They think they own the place and they do.

'How can I be of service?' Pedro asked. He sat opposite us at an outside table. We prayed the heavens wouldn't open. He clasped his hands together as he rested his elbows upon the table, his movements slow, calm and with purpose. I had the impression we weren't his first clients. We conversed in Spanish, Mark sat quiet as I had instructed.

'We heard you can source wild boar.' I stated.

'Yes but for what reason?' he asked, opening his weathered hands. I could see they were calloused, probably years of working in the fields.

'Mark has never tried wild boar,' I fibbed, at the time forgetting he had briefly tried it on one occasion, 'and we have a few get-togethers with friends coming up,' I answered. Pedro smiled. He was a seasoned hunter, and he spoke about the boars roaming in and out of towns like feral cats. In large cities such as Barcelona, boar populations have soared to such an extent that the authorities have no choice but to capture and put them down. Now they're posing a threat to people by raiding bins and people are feeding them encouraging them to forage in more built up areas. You know when your car hits a wild boar; it will most likely be a write off.

'*Pueden ser tan grandes como 200kg*,' Pedro continued.

'He says they can be around 200kg,' I translated to Mark.

The Spanish wild boar is different from its domestic relative; their coat is dense, bristly and grey-brown in colour. Their canine teeth form tusks, and they hunt by night. They're fast runners and strong swimmers.

'Wild boar have become a huge problem, especially since the pandemic. They're camping in towns and villages,' Pedro continued.

'So why isn't it more common to eat wild boar? We searched everywhere. The local butchers looked at us like we wanted to buy drugs. It probably would have been easier.'

'Not really that common around here. You would have to head towards Albacete,' Pedro said. 'I haven't hunted this year, but I have a freezer full if you want some?'

'That would be great.'

'Meet me here, next Tuesday, same time.'

Pedro ended up being a very nice chap. He handed us two plastic shopping bags the following Tuesday evening.

'Without a fridge/freezer, it's going to smell like a morgue,' Mark crinkled his nose as we placed them into the boot. As we shut the door, a couple of English folk that we had met a few weeks back walked over. Rob must have been in his eighties, and we had only met them a couple of times, each with the holding of my hand, the sniff of my hair, the tickle of my neck. You know the normal geriatric creeper that every village has. Mark thought it was funny. As for Rob's wife Sally, she was a dead ringer for Catherine Tate's Nan.

'Howdy, you two,' Rob grinned. 'Fancy seeing you two around here! Grab a drink?'

'We were…' Mark started and I jabbed him in the side.

'We'd love to,' I beamed.

Rob and Sally had moved to the area twenty years ago. Now retired they spend their time bar hopping. We asked them where a good place to buy wild boar would be, because rendezvousing with Pedro wasn't ideal.

'Wild boar?' Rob erupted. 'Remember when we asked for wild boar, Sally?' he laughed.

'Ahh don't remind me!' his wife grimaced, but was ignored.

'Years ago we asked a hunter for a wild boar and after a joyous evening, half pissed, we got back into our car to find two bloody bodies thrown into the boot of our car.'

'Good grief. What did you do?' Mark asked.

'We drove home. I didn't know what to do with them. Sally wanted no involvement. So, I rang Javi, the gardener, to come and sort them out. And sort them out he did. But he left the heads and all sorts for me to dispose of.'

'I'm telling you, Rob. He did it on purpose because you didn't pay him for the work he did the previous week. You had it coming,' she smiled in an irritatingly conceited way.

'And he helped himself to some of it. Bastard.'

'Did you eat it?' I beckoned.

Rob's voice escalated a few decibels, and he gesticulated frantically, waving his hands and arms around in front of his face. He exclaimed, 'Not right away. But when we did, it was bloody lovely!'

Many years ago, Mark and I were invited to a birthday party at the Maserof; a winery museum and private wine club. It is a non-profit philanthropic and cultural association that anyone can join for free as a volunteer member. While we were enthralled in the conversation with Pedro, the memory of the birthday party had slipped our minds. We had drunk too many wine samples that day.

As a volunteer member, you agree to participate once a year in the meetings and restoration of the museum to conserve the historical heritage of the Roman Villa; Maserof. The museum is located in an enclave between mountains Sierra de Bernia, the Montgo, Costera del Ferrer, and the Tossal del Navarro. It allows you to witness original pieces from the Roman era right up to the 19th century. The dining room is very rustic, with walls adorned with furniture from the 12th to the 19th century. A huge open fire place, large beams and tiles original to the Roman times add to its charm. You can also discover the original tank from such times where grapes were trod on and still to this day continue to be trod on by candlelight for members and friends of members, usually around September – harvest time. Mark admired it as 'very, very rustic.'

'Fortunately the bathrooms are a little more up to date. No poo sticks in there. I'm not sure whether I'm grateful or slightly disappointed,' I rubbed my hands together.

'Poo sticks?'

'Yes...Romans wiped their arses with sea sponges that were wrapped on the end of a stick. Every community bathroom had one. After using it, patrons would rinse and leave it for the next person. I'd have thought with all the effort they had made, they wouldn't have skimped on the finer things,' I shrugged.

'Like a modern day toilet brush, only it was for your bum hole?'

'Exactly,' I acknowledged.

Speaking of poo sticks, Sheila had informed us that Maria had dropped off some gifts for us for when we next saw Sheila; toilet brushes. They look new, Sheila said, although they're not that clean, so Sheila said she would toss them. I wondered what might have been going through Maria's mind when she decided oh Mark and Abbie would love these... Her heart is in the right place and I treasure my house-warming goodie bag of recipe books.

Here, at the Maserof, we listened to artisanal ways of wine production, tasted stinging nettle soup, watched the traditional method of making soap with caustic soda, and dined on roasted wild boar caught that day. But as glorious as it sounds, our inviter had other plans of accidently throwing a glass of wine into the fire causing it to erupt like an angry volcano, and we were all asked to leave shortly after dessert. Mark and I have never been back since.

The following morning, two large white plastic bags sat inside our sink. Hesitantly, Mark opened one up, crinkling his nose at the slight whiff. Death was ineffable, indescribable, but very present. Mark twanged on a pair of Marigolds and withdrew the bag's contents, slamming a large set of ribs onto the countertop.

'Oh, Jesus,' he said.

'It looks human.'

'How do you know what human ribs look like?' he queried.

'CSI,' I shrugged.

'Well, it's got two chances.'

Our wild boar

Wild boar roast

When cooking wild boar you can essentially treat it like a 2 lb joint of pork, because in most ways it is. Always make sure that where you purchase your boar from it has been <u>frozen</u> and <u>vet checked.</u> The mantra with wild boar is to cook slow and low.

1 Over proof tray
1 joint of wild boar – ribs / loin / leg
1 onion, chopped into quarters
3 large garlic cloves
3 rough length cut carrots
½ kilo baby potatoes
6 mushrooms
Splash of red wine
1 sprig of Rosemary
Salt and Pepper

Method

Add the wild boar to your cold oven tray. Dice the onion into quarters and add to each corner of the tray.

Place whole garlic cloves evenly spaced into the tray with your peeled and large rough cut carrots.

Add the whole, unpeeled baby potatoes.

Splash your red wine. It's your prerogative how much you add as it's completely arbitrary depending on your taste.

This dish can also be done without red wine.
Add salt and pepper and place your sprig of Rosemary on top of your meat.
Cover with tin foil so it's sealed.
Bake at 150 degrees Celsius for 4 hours – checking every hour.
Add whole mushrooms and place back into the over for another hour and a half.

Did you know?

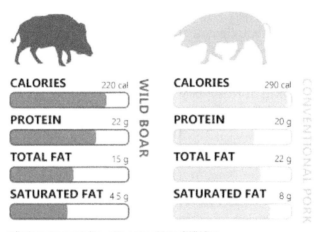

CALORIES 220 cal
PROTEIN 22 g
TOTAL FAT 15 g
SATURATED FAT 4.5 g

WILD BOAR

CALORIES 290 cal
PROTEIN 20 g
TOTAL FAT 22 g
SATURATED FAT 8 g

CONVENTIONAL PORK

*All information provided on a 100g serving of Ground Wild Boar
**Source usda.gov

Eating healthier has been on many people's minds lately. Moving to a more rural and natural way of living has made us both pay more attention to what we're eating. Although hesitant at first about trying Wild Boar, we realised it was a much healthier alternative to traditional meat, especially when nowadays we don't really know what we're buying when it's carefully and beautifully packaged.

Mark divided the meat into several more manageable pieces. I placed a set of ribs and the loin into my oven tray, coating them in a generous amount of salt and pepper, and a drizzle of olive oil.

Then, I added my root vegetables and other ingredients. After several hours of cooking, I was surprised by how tender and tasty it was. There was no gaminess, just a unique and bold flavour that is akin to a cross between pork and beef. It was almost like the end piece of a good roasted beef joint that's packed full of flavour. The boar's flavour is largely due to their diet of grass, nuts and shrubs.

However, don't stick to just what I suggest. Use it as a guide and adjust it to suit your taste-buds and what is available to you. Cooking should be stress-free and something to be enjoyed with friends and family.

CHAPTER 17

"Whatever goes upon two legs is an enemy"
George Orwell Animal Farm

The Land Rover's tyres obliterated the dirt track further as we ascended to the house, the dust cloud pluming either side. We hadn't had any rain for weeks, everything was so dry. The land looked like the fields were about to erupt into flame, they simmered with the heat. The once green pastures were now barren, and all the flora shriveled from the baking sun. We hustled inside to escape the cankerous heat as our skin prickled with a needling stabbing sensation as the moisture was sucked out of our pores. There was nothing ambrosial about the summer heat here, only the blasphemous intentions of nature's desire to kill us and everything brave enough to challenge it.

We'd heard the Spanish countryside had harsher sunlight than the coast, what we didn't know was how it felt like a desert. The wind howled, birds cawed, eagles screeched and then silence. It was almost deafening.

We hadn't been at the property for long, just a few months really, everything was still very new. We were yet to install electricity or a mains source of water. The house, inside had what's called an *ajibe* – a built in water tank. It took up some 25sqm and straight away Mark and I decided that wasn't ideal. It could be accessed in the upstairs bedroom by lifting a hatch – God forbid you fall out of bed; you'll end up with more than a cold shower. For now, we made do with a tub. There is no real distinction as to the specific size that a bathtub needs to be, to be considered small; however, this one took the biscuit. One can only suggest that for this Spanish family who built the house that life without a tub simply wasn't worth living. As Mark put it, you build what you're used to. This was an old Spanish family living in a country house after all. This was a country whose southern part is mostly desert, an extension of North Africa's Sahara Desert. Even now, the countryside is teeming with wild rosemary and the coast is lined with palm trees. Even to this day, many country homes lack running water. It wouldn't surprise me that in this very house there was once a copper kept warm by the large open fireplace. One of the outbuildings still had the old scrubbing board and I imagined the family hanging out their laundry on a cold, winter's day with it freezing stiff taking on the form of the clothes line. Had Juan as a boy been brought up with such a bathtub? Had the installation of the tiny-tub been an upgrade, or a financial make-do? After all, there was room for a normal sized bathtub, even a shower.

I've enjoyed a few soaks in my time. Taking a

warm bath with scented candles can not only have great physical but mental health benefits too. But if anything can strengthen your relationship, it's seeing your partner naked, squatting, knees up to their chest whilst you douse them down with a pesticide pump filled with soapy, warm water.

'Turn around,' I had said as I pumped away and pulled the trigger, sprinkling water over Mark's naked body.

'Do my arse,' Mark indicated with his finger, and I sprayed. 'No! Closer…' he suggested.

I grabbed onto one of his cheeks, pulled it apart so I could rid his nooks and crannies of soap, and I refrained from saying a word.

'It's not like pulling apart a cheese sandwich, just get the soap off,' Mark reached behind him.

'OK, wash your own bum, you're not decrepit,' I retorted.

I wouldn't say Mark was particularly comfortable in his own skin when baring it in all its glory. Everyone has body anxiety, and he is no exception. Fortunately, he spends less time in front of a mirror than I do, and that was saying something. However, with his dwindling eyesight it was up to me to trim his eyebrow hairs before he grew his own set of shades. I drew the line when it came to more personal areas.

In the early days of moving to the house, I had to get used to the fact that shaving wasn't going to be a daily occurrence, OK it never really was, but with this tiny tub it was near impossible, and too darn cold to even try. You would only really get enough hot water boiled on the stove to wash the necessities: face, pits, tits and bits. Forget long, hot showers, we didn't have the water pressure for that. Forget waxing. Forget pumicing. It was of no real surprise that within a few months of moving to the property I began to look like some unruly teenager, my hair taking on its own permed appearance as the humidity set in, and this time I couldn't blame it on stress.

However, Spanish country homes tend to be summer getaways, where the locals move out of the town to escape the hordes of people that flock in for the fiestas, and I feel we could all learn from our Spanish neighbours, because television, and the internet don't seem to be the focus of family gatherings. One might wonder how anyone survived in our home and many others with connecting power to a car battery, the lack of a fridge, TV, gas bottles, but they do. As Juan, the old farmer whose dark, leathery skin signified a working life outdoors, had once told us, they would sit outside in the front, right in the middle of the wilderness with a bottle of red, a board of cured meat and cheese, shelling peanuts, and chat away until the early morning hours.

"La cabra montesa..." The Spanish Ibex", he would say, "would come down from the mountain in search of food. They would walk right past us,

and eat everything in sight." Which we later found out was true when our beautiful Ivy climber was suddenly missing all its lower leaves. We've seen a couple of specimens, well, one looked like a suspiciously dubious scraggy creature, and although destructive, we feel honoured to have seen one so soon. The animals have over the years aroused somewhat of a mythological attraction. In the early twentieth century apparently only twelve were counted. They were on the verge of disappearing forever, and thanks to the monarch with the royal preserve, the population multiplied and poachers were paid to stop hunting them. Now, if we're lucky we can witness them defying the laws of gravity right on our doorstep. Time has been too kind to the Spanish Ibex, with no real natural predators there are now too many; Madrid alone has some 6,000 individuals, whereas the optimum number being around 1,500 and 2,000 animals. Juan advised us to be vigilant as now with so many animals populating one area there is an outbreak of scabies.

The Iberian wolf, like the Ibex, was also hunted to near extinction in Spain. Shepherds in the northern parts of Spain are now warning of their return. However, the Iberian wolf population has enjoyed a resurgence since the 1970s, thanks to new hunting regulations. Their numbers have reached around 2,000 specimens mainly around Castilla, Leon, Galicia, Cantabria and Asturias.

These two stood in the road and defied gravity by skipping along the rock face alongside the road as we drove past.

CHAPTER 18

Sometimes you have just got to say Cluck it!

Today, Duncan was giving us a hand; we were demolishing and removing the old pizza oven that was collapsing, and in time would have pulled the adjacent building down with it. We planned on converting the space to a BBQ area , after all, Spain is for outdoor living, and we had ideas of enlivening the area with various colours of native fauna, with seating positioned to capitalise on the outstanding view of the mountain that sits back from the village of Zarra. Zarra only has a population of 500, having increased slightly mainly due to the influx of British residents because of its old world timelessness with the majority of the houses dating back some 400 years.

The day had a vibrant blue sky that was as clear as glass. Dust devils swirled around us as we mixed cement, and my face began to split from the dehydration. I gazed out towards the terrain, and with the flecks of cement dust that spat from the machine sucking any moisture from my lips, I started to feel like the vultures next meal. Gliding over head, they moved without much effort. They didn't look like they could have a wingspan of nearly ten feet (3 metres) and I wasn't prepared to find out. Having moved to the country and the abundance of wild life, I had taken a great interest in learning about our surrounding inhibitors.

'What's the matter with you, girl?' Mark shouted as he walked towards me with his wheelbarrow.

'I'm just so hot.'

'Surprised you're not used to it. Oh vultures! Looks like they're soaring the thermals,' he smiled.

'Looks like the Griffon Vulture,' I added but Mark took no mind.

Together with the black vulture; a large scavenger having a wingspan of nearly three metres and a weight of up to ten kilograms, the Griffon Vulture was almost comparable in size, and it soared above us. A spectacular sight bestowed before us, and it made the expression "vulture" a phrase used to insult someone who preys on the weak, seem almost cruel. Known to fly hundreds of kilometers in search for food, these notable birds dedicate almost 50% of their life to nest building and taking care of their young. As monogamous animals, it breaks my heart that mortality rates according to The Guardian, for Aragón and Navarra showed 1,387 Griffon Vultures, 6 Egyptian vultures, 30 Golden Eagles, 58 short-toed snake eagles and 76 Red Kites died in wind farms in these two regions between 2020 and 2022 alone.

They are recognisable by their dark silhouette appearing almost rectangular with its head far extended. It is abundant in Spain's forestall areas, and lives alongside the Spanish Imperial Eagle. The Griffon Vulture was a beautiful sight, seeing as we are surrounded by Olive groves. Usually, vultures prefer open areas with few trees and livestock as they enjoy feasting on the corpses of the varying species of ungulates that it co-exists with.

In Castilla-La Mancha, the autonomous community comprising the provinces of Albacete, Ciudad Real, Cuenca, Guadalajara and Toledo, has black vulture nests in its woodland areas that are abundant with oak and cork oaks with altitudes of around 850-900m above sea level, and on slopes with a 15-25% angle. The Castilla-La Mancha also boasts the second largest population of this particular vulture.

Since our move, we have witnessed a great deal of partridge too – each time a covey running off like little old women as we drove back and forth to the property.

'Does anyone want a drink? I think I'll have a break,' I emptied the cement into the barrow and poured in a bucket of water to prevent it drying out, and I turned the machine to a low spin.

'Yeah, Dunc and I will have a Coca Cola if we've got some,' Mark answered.

'I guess we'll have to keep an eye on the raptors if we're going to get chickens,' I stated as I handed the boys their refreshments. It was common knowledge that various types of bird of prey, the Eurasian Owl being no exception, were snatching unattended chickens.

'Chickens?' Duncan interrupted. 'Fresh, Spanish chicken fajitas on the menu then?'

'Fajitas are Mexican and no, we won't be eating our chickens. They'll be part of the family,' I corrected.

Sure enough, the following week we bought our four hens: Eggatha Christie, Whoopi, Jabba the Hen and Attila the Hen. It took Mark and I a couple of days to refurbish the old coop. We rendered the exterior walls, painted it sparkling white and gave the doorframe a lick of paint in the colour of lush, green grass. Inside, we painted the walls, added more soil and erected a little wood cabin for them to sleep in at night. These hens were part of our family. There wasn't really a chance I'd have let our new hens see Juan's old slaughter table and ten inch blade.

'I need you to pee around the coop,' I gestured with my finger.

'Excuse me?' Mark questioned.

'Urine, it's to deter the foxes.'

'Then you do it.'

'No, I can't. It has to be male urine. It's not an old wives tale; there must be hundreds of foxes around here. The wee rumour is true. Come on.'

Mark looked side-to-side and unzipped his trousers. He parted his legs and hoicked it out, hopping from one foot to the next as he waved it around like a hosepipe.

'What are you doing?' I queried.

'Pissing on our patch just like you asked.'

'You don't need to cover everything!'

'I just want to make sure Mr Fox thinks twice about hanging around here. No different than what lions do when they spray up bushes. I've seen Daddy cat do it,' he zipped up.

'Lions also defecate conspicuously. Are you going to leave one of those too?' I suggested.

'Don't be daft.'

Mark wanted a cockerel. I believe Mark felt there was an unfair male to female ratio in our household. His alliance consisting of an eleven-year-old deaf bulldog, a twenty-year old street cat called Daddy who enjoys bitty and Thai green curry from time to time as well as many other gastronomic choices, and my fourteen-year-old, knicker drawer raiding cat who, if he was human would be a small boy wearing a protective leather hat with people calling him special. So, Mark thought the addition of a robust and handsome cockerel would somehow even the playing field. After discussions with our local supplier of construction material and JCB driver, and his methods of asserting dominance within *his* flock, I reiterated to Mark that somehow I couldn't quite see him going in to the coop, and grabbing his cock mid flight, giving it a good shake and saying, *'Yo jefe, tu no.'* I'm the boss, not you.

Duncan also told us that there wasn't an Indian

restaurant within an hour and a half drive. And if Mark and I knew that before we signed the deeds, it might just have been a deal breaker. Fortunately, Duncan had dropped into conversation that the local Kebab shop had once catered privately for desperate Brits like us. That was something we would have to enquire about. For the meantime, I came across this recipe, which, I have to say, turned out bloody marvelous. It satiated our Indian cuisine desires and the best surprise of the century was the homemade chapattis.

Mark and I aren't vegetarians, but we do try and live a healthier lifestyle by incorporating many vegetables into our daily diet, even if I have to disguise them by chopping them up into very small pieces. I'm often cooking vegetarian & vegan meals, turning to Indian recipes and spices as a good source of inspiration. One of our dear friends, John, is a vegetarian, and has a cast-iron stomach. We met him through our business and were captivated by his life as a guitarist, composer, author and arranger. John, this once Neil Diamond from the '70s, had his debut in London, 1968 for his first solo concert at the Purcell Room, Royal Festival Hall and it launched him into the London musical world. He, at this time, was making guitar recordings for the television series The Strauss Family with the London Symphony Orchestra.

He is in his very late seventies now, and has extensive travel knowledge of south Asia. He says he's survived to this day with mosquitoes biting his eyelids shut, swarms of army ants eating his toes, and swears blind that chillies are the secret to a strong stomach and why eating street food should always be spicy or avoided.

In 1972, he recorded his first solo recording with publisher Belwin Mills and subsequently received a gold album award in 1983. During 1972 and 1973, becoming a member of the Royal Shakespeare company, he made the world tour with Peter Brook's production of Midsummer Night's Dream, and it was during this year of travels, John's interest in music from the Latin Americas flourished. John's catalogue includes composing and performing original music for Alby James' production of Romeo and Juliet. You may have even heard of the 1990 Jonathan Porrit's BBC TV production Where On Earth Are We Going? For which, John also composed and performed the music. As a revered master of Latin Guitar, he has also performed at venues as varied as the Queen Elizabeth Hall, London to Ronnie Scott's Jazz Club. And as Victor Canning once put in his novel Birdcage, I too find myself with a glass of wine, listening to John's music on occasion and thinking, "Every note *is* golden."

At a restaurant – on the coast, Mark and I had ordered our usual; Chicken Tikka Dhansak and a Chicken Tikka Masala. John ordered a vegetable curry – Vindaloo hot. He also asked for a side of ghost chillies, picking at them like roasted peanuts. I like hot food, but I do have limits.

However, although abundant on the coast, curry houses just aren't the same here in Spain. And in rural Spain, you're lucky if there is one within a two hour drive. Here is one of our homemade favourites; a mild, naturally vegan and budget friendly concoction. Add the chillies to your desire.

It's taken the edge off our curry craves many times.

Chickpea, Coconut and Spinach Dhal

Dhal is an Indian dish traditionally eaten with flat breads, rotis, chapattis or rice. Here's my recipe that's quick to make, extremely popular, vegan and nutritious.

Naturally Vegan – Dairy free –Gluten free – Budget friendly

1 saucepan
3 garlic cloves
2cm peeled and finely chopped fresh ginger
3 medium sized finely chopped spring onions
10 cherry tomatoes
1 400g tin coconut milk
200g cooked lentils
200g cooked chickpeas
2 tbsp curry powder
2 tsp cumin
1 tsp tumeric
1 lime juiced
2 tsp chilli powder / 1 fresh finely chopped chilli (optional)
Handful of fresh spinach
1 cup of raisins (optional)

Method

Add a small amount of oil to a large sauce and lightly fry without burning the garlic, ginger, spring onion.

Add curry powder, cumin, turmeric and coconut milk. Stir until mixed. Keep on a medium heat.

Add lentils, chickpeas, and cut 5 cherry tomatoes in half then add them to the pan.

Simmer for ten minutes then add spinach and remainder of whole cherry tomatoes. Add raisins.

Simmer for three minutes and serve.

This curry was one of the first recipes that went into *All my fucking recipes,* and is still cooked for guests to this day, because we still haven't found a curry house. This one-pot vegan recipe is surprisingly full of flavour, is budget friendly and will take you around forty-five minutes from prep to serve, tops. Although there is loads of room for your own creative twist, I cannot emphasise enough the use of lime, and in my humble opinion an absolute essential ingredient to this recipe. Once you have perfected your curry base by experimenting with the amounts of the ingredients to suit your palate, you can explore with a variety of flavours. For instance, you can add lamb or pork, a can of tomatoes, a chilli, chilli powder, broccoli instead of spinach, and a handful of raisins. This will give your dish a rich and complex flavour profile.

Spanish love their chickpeas and they are a common ingredient in the Mediterranean diet. If you find you have left over chickpeas and spinach from making the curry then try this *Espinacas con Garbanzos* (Spinach and Chickpeas) recipe.

If you happen to reside in a remote area of Spain and are concerned about missing out on your favourite curry, fret not! Indian cuisine is surprisingly easy to replicate and offers ample room for experimentation. However, the most astonishing discovery was the chapatti. Who would have thought that a simple mixture of flour and water could satiate one's bread cravings?

Spinach and Chickpeas,
Espinacas con Garbanzos

*An easy traditional dish from southern Spain,
chickpea and spinach spiced with cumin,, common
as a tapa in Seville, Spain.*

*Naturally Vegan – Dairy free –Gluten free –
Budget friendly*

3 tbsp virgin olive oil
3 garlic cloves
3 tbsp sweet paprika
1 bag or 6 cups of fresh spinach leaves
½ cup of water
1 400g jar of cooked chickpeas
Salt and pepper

Method

*Dice the garlic cloves and lightly fry without
burning with the olive oil. Add the paprika, stir and
slowly add the spinach until wilted. Add the cooked
chickpeas. Cook for 5 minutes, salt and pepper to
taste. You might want to add more paprika.*

The moors were the first to introduce spinach as
well as many other ingredients to Spain in the time
of Al-Andalus, a term used by historians for what

was then former Islamic states in Spain, Portugal and France that occupied most of the Peninsula from 711 CE until the collapse of the Spanish Umayyad dynasty in early 11th Century. So, this dish is a reminder of Spain's history. Spain love meat, but it's not impossible to live a more vegan lifestyle if you chose to, and if living a more Mediterranean diet is something that appeals to you then you can accomplish both vegan and easy on the wallet with this simple dish. I like to use jarred, cooked chickpeas and fresh spinach, but either canned or jarred chickpeas and frozen spinach works just fine.

As we continued working on the property, I realised my passion for cooking had reignited. I found myself flipping through pages of recipe books excited at the idea of cooking for people. I'd just have to keep Mark out of the kitchen. If he so much as smelt garlic, I'd get *the* look, even though pretty much everything I cook included garlic.

'Garlic,' he would say, as if the one-worded comment was meant to render some kind of meaning.

'Yes, garlic, and ginger, and chilli,' I would smile whilst stirring.

He would bend over the pan, and stare deep into my eyes without saying a word.

'Look, Mark, you eat everything I put in front of

you,' I would state. He would then stand, glaring at the food, at me, at the food again and generally come out with some half-wit comment that would render him being tea towel whooped out of the kitchen.

'Is my arse going to look like a Japanese flag in the morning?'

'No. These are fresh chillies, not as hot as chilli powder. Now go away.'

I busied myself in the kitchen as Mark ate some Russian Salad I had whipped up the day before, and as I lowered the baking tray into the oven, a loud smash was heard. Startled, I ran into the back room where I had left Mark, only to find his cat on top of the table with a gherkin in his mouth.

'Mark!!'

'What?' he replied from his workshop.

'Get your bloody cat out of here,' I scorned.

'What's he done now?'

'He's stealing food.'

'But, I didn't leave any food,' Mark wondered.

'The pickle, he ate the pickle!'

'That's my boy,' Mark laughed.

Homemade chapatti

2 cups of flour
1 cup of water
Brush with butter (without butter if vegan and typically how we would have it)

Method

Add two cups of flour to a bowl through a sieve to remove any large clumps. Slowly add room temperature water and mix until you have pliable dough.

Divide into 1 ½ inch balls. Flour a surface and roll each ball into a thin pancake.

Heat a non stick frying over a high heat – you want to make sure your frying pan is hot so it cooks the outside and doesn't dry out your chapattis.

Carefully lay one chapatti at a time into your dry hot frying pan, toss when you can see the typically spotted browning.

Serve hot with or without a brush of butter.

Homemade Naan Bread

1 7g sachet of yeast
½ cup of warm water
2 tsp castor sugar
2 cups of white flour
½ cup of plain yogurt
½ tsp salt
1 tbsp olive oil
3 tbsp melted butter / preferably ghee
½ tsp baking powder

Method

Put the warm water into a small bowl and sprinkle over the yeast + 1 tsp of sugar. Leave until frothy – around 10 minutes.

In a larger bowl, add the flour, 1 tsp of sugar, salt and baking powder. Mix well. Make a well in the middle and slowly add the melted butter and yogurt, then the yeast mixture. Combine by folding the outsides into the middle. Add more flour if the mixture is too wet.

Knead the dough on a floured surface, returning the ball to the bowl, cover and leave to rise for 1 hour or until doubled in size.

Divide into six balls roughly golf ball size, and roll each dough to form a tear drop shape.

Heat a non stick frying pan and dry fry each tear drop until evening browned on both sides.

Remove from the pan and place onto a plate, brush with butter. Continue to stack your naan breads, and serve immediately.

CHAPTER 19

Fowl play with chicken shit bingo

Duncan looked depressed. He had just returned from a 10 day break on the coast. His daughters had lectured him that one day a woman will end his life.

'Duncan, you must think sensibly, where around here are you going to get genital warts lasered off your donk? Mark asked.

'I don't think they've got anything!' Duncan replied. 'But maybe you're right. My daughters say any one of these women could be a serial killer. She might chop me up. Men have to be scared too!'

Mark and I looked at each other. Duncan wasn't a small man, certainly of average build, and we thought it unlikely that a woman was lurking on a dating app to lure someone like Duncan into her unsuspecting trap, to you know, chop him up.

'They're out there. Man-haters,' he nodded convincingly. Of course, it isn't unheard of and Duncan was certainly increasing his chances of having a bunny boiled on his stove.

He looked into his lap. 'But most women on the coast are either pissed as farts or fucking ugly,' he shrugged.

'Maybe you're just looking in the wrong place, Dunc?' I asked.

'This one, from La Marina…' he began… 'bit older than me, about 69 I reckon. I only met her once, in Benidorm. She's not really my type but you know, you can tell when someone likes ya?'

'Aha…' Mark nodded. I'd already put a brew on, knowing we were in for another story.

When I returned with three mugs of tea I asked, 'Can't you just watch BoobTube?'

'What's that?'

'You know… porn…'

'Oh no, I find that is really degrading….I don't know why I shagged her,' he continued. Mark and I glanced at one another and sipped our teas. 'Well, I didn't really shag her, just got a nosh. I'm surprised she didn't chew it off. This time, we just started talking. She'd been watching this program Fake Date or something which is just sex. So, I sexted her but nothing. She didn't reply, and you know why, don't you?' Duncan looked at us like we knew the answer.

'No…why?' I asked.

'Because, it was day time; come night, she comes alive. *Really randy!* She said, "Come round Thursday. Stay over." She had a BBQ with the neighbour Friday and she sells cream on the *rastro* at the weekend. She said, "I'll change the sheets downstairs *and* my sheets." Also told me she had massive tits but had had them reduced. Now they're just white because she doesn't get them out. I told her I'd find them easily in the dark then,' he scoffed.

Pretty much every time we see Duncan, we're enlightened about modern day dating.

We had been living at the property for near on six months by now, and the building work was coming along lovely. Mark and I had done most of the work ourselves, including re-felting leaky rooftops. We had managed to install Solar without too much hassle by a couple of Dutch brothers: Cas and Wilbert, who were recommended to us by the estate agent.

Installing a solar system meant we minimised our chances of regular power outages, which often can last for several hours, and is very common throughout Spain. And it's surprising with a country so vigilant on wild fires just how many country homes with appliances are not earthed out. It's not uncommon to find plug sockets near water supplies and in bathrooms, and if you're connected to the mains, power is often interrupted by storms. The average electricity current is 220V, unlike the UK's 240V, in some areas Spain has it as low as 200V, so most UK electrical appliances work just fine. However, in some older properties it is still possible to find a 110V installation, and in our case a 12V installation that ran off a car battery that powered the lights. It's not encouraged to use a plug adaptor for foreign appliances although many do, as they get hot and become a fire hazard especially the ones from the Chinese bazaars.

We aptly named the brothers "The Booby Brothers" as their surname Borst literally means breast when translated into English from their native language, and the four of us have become quite good friends.

Recently, Yesenia, Mark and I attended one of their infamous burger evenings where, Wilbert, who Mark and I now call Wilma because of his feminine house-making and culinary skills, made some of the best burgers we have ever tasted. And Yesenia found it most amusing that although she offered to wash up that evening, Wilma claimed that, although they lived in the campo they weren't primitive, and did indeed have a dishwasher. *Not sure what he was trying to say here, as we do not have a dishwasher...*

'What's he doing?' I asked Cas as Wilma walked around banging a saucepan, in a fifty meter radius from where we were sat. Cas answered, 'Letting the animals know we're here. They'll be attracted to the smell.'

'You don't have bloody coyotes around here, we're not in North America,' I retorted. 'The best you would get among these wooded trees is getting rammed by some ruminant.'

Everyone huddled closer, even the chicken that lay under the table looked decidedly nervous at the commotion.

'Another burger anyone, I have made 16,' Wilma grinned across the table as he walked back towards us.

With their mum and aunt, there were only seven of us. '16? Who else did you invite?' Mark laughed.

Cas chimed in… 'No one, but we usually eat 3 or 4 each.'

'You're the skinny one and you eat more than I do!' exclaimed Wilma who grabbed his A cups and said, 'but tonight I'll just stick to the one burger, I'm trying to get my A away.'

'You're going to scare your chicken with all that banging,' Mark pointed.

'She'll be alright,' he said as he lifted the cloth. 'She's been there for 3 days now. Looked a little under the weather and she's not laid for a couple of days either. Might end up in the pot,' Cas shrugged.

'Oh no, she's gorgeous. Don't do that. She's such a striking, sandy colour too. If she's not laying she can earn her keep in other ways.'

Everyone looked at me in bewilderment.

'Like what/how?' asked Mark.

'Chicken Shit Bingo!' I replied.

Wilma burst into laughter. 'Did she just say what I think she said?' he asked his brother.

'And what in god's name is that?' Mark raised his brow.

'Well, it's not that much of a mystery is it? It is as the name entails. Bingo and chicken shit. Your number is called when the chicken drops one on a numbered square. If that number matches your ticket, hey presto, you win.'

'Are you for real, babe?' Yesenia looked concerned.

'Of course. In fact, sod you lot. We're going to do it, aren't we Mark?'

'Hey, what?'

'Write that down, so we don't forget,' I pointed.

Cas shook his head and I smiled. 'You must have heard of Cat Shit Coffee?'

'What in God's name is that?' Wilma implored.

Mark dismissed it and claimed it was something rich people liked to drink.

'Coffee made from the coffee beans that are gathered from the Civet's feces. There is some fancy name for it, but I prefer the more vulgar term Cat Shit Coffee,' I exclaimed.

'Of course you do,' Cas laughed.

'Even though it's around $10 a cup, it's a bargain compared to Elephant poop coffee.'

'Stop it!' Wilma laughed.

'You like your coffee black…hmm Black Ivory Coffee with notes of chocolate, malt, spice and a hint of grass. No average cup o'joe, but don't knock it until you try it. I even read someone calling it a Crapuccino.'

'No wonder you drink tea!' Yesenia grimaced.

CHAPTER 20

"It's not about your resources, it's about your resourcefulness" Tony Robbins

We didn't really miss electricity. When we moved to the house, the average temperature sat around 15 degrees Celsius, and we made do with the old-fashioned larder where we stored food prior to its use. We also had a gas cooker and a BBQ.

Country life and living off-grid was off to a promising start. Moving to a property that is off-grid can seem like a daunting task, and it's taken a little while to get accustomed to filling our water bottles up at the village fountain for washing up and boiling, instead of using water from our water deposit. It's also always best to buy bottled drinking water than drink straight from the tap although, tap water in Spain is allegedly one of the best in Europe, which as a rule I tend to disagree with as water all over Spain varies in quality. And whilst if you're a seasoned Spanish tap water drinker, you might not notice the odour or taste the minerals it contains, it can sometimes upset the more sensitive stomachs of tourists that aren't used to it. In the coastal regions the water can contain sand or sediment which gives it a gritty taste. It's always planted that seed of doubt in my mind and when water is less than a euro per 8 litres to buy, it's a no brainer. More often, many residents resort to water filters that filter out the chlorine and other contaminants, but either way the subject of water is not something to worry about in general.

The unusual abundance of rainfall we had had provided life all around. The grounds were teeming with green weeds and everywhere we looked sprouted green grass – even in the height of summer thanks to the sporadic rain. It was like a green carpet, everywhere you looked there were mountains, whose peaks were hundreds of meters high, dotted with pine trees, the red flaking bark of the arbutus tree, thick, woody, wild Rosemary, and despite the harsh, dry days, the Jucar river flowed stretching almost fourteen kilometers through landscapes of indescribable beauty.

Countless birds sat atop our pine trees singing their melodic symphonies, and my heart began to grow for wanting to plant more organically grown vegetables and eat tomatoes freshly picked from the vine, chillies, and potatoes and so on.

In just six months, Mark and I realised just how quickly time was flying, but even six months on we still didn't have a shower.

So, there we were one morning, me with a head full of hair dye, bent over the tiny-tub and pesticide pump. Mark was rinsing tepid water over me determined to rid the red colourant out of the previous dye attempt. I'm not sure when I started to take a dislike to Mark, but over the years I'd learnt to love him like Charlie loves Wonka bars. I often wondered if this was it, as good as a relationship would get, and as I bent over the edge of the tub, he prodded me in my side.

'What's that?' he asked.

I tilted my head to the side and answered, 'My rib.'

'That's a well-covered rib. If I was at a BBQ I'd *want* that rib!'

I'm not sure what happened from the beginning of our relationship to now, and I sighed, hypothetically patting myself on the back. I'd have done less years for murder.

'All right, George Clooney…'

I'd just wrapped it up when the cats scuttled upstairs, terrified of the raucous sounds outside; two men wandering around our car and garden. Mark ran outside topless, figuratively beating his chest like a silver-backed mountain gorilla. I followed suit. There wasn't much time to change out of my silk chemise and remove the brown blotches off my face, it wasn't how I'd usually see members of the public, but Mark ran outside without a thought in mind and he didn't speak Spanish.

I threw on a tee-shirt and shorts, and continued our discussion outside. It appeared the two brothers owned a small plot adjacent to ours at the back of the garden, and they wanted to know if we were interested in buying it. I said that a toot of the horn would have sufficed, but they said they had given us the courtesy of walking up to our windows and making noise rather than driving across our garden. All was good after a good conversation; we realised they weren't related to the ex-owners of the house but did inform us that the reason the house underwent some renovation was because the lady's boyfriend had fallen asleep with a cigarette in his hand, and it set the place on fire, with him inside. He burnt alive. And there we were admiring the fact we were lucky the property had a decent roof, and, in some areas fairly new rooftops.

Spaghetti alla Carbonara
The Spanish *Twist*

3 tbsp olive oil
2 tbsp butter (if salted use less salt when seasoning)
4 medium sized eggs
100g grated Grano Padano/ Parmesan
100g grated Manchego cheese
150g diced Jamon Serrano
400g spaghetti
Ground salt and black pepper
1 tsp Paprika

Method

Combine the oil and butter in a frying pan over a low-medium heat. Adding the oil will prevent the butter from burning.

Add the diced Jamon Serrano and fry until lightly crispy then set aside.

Add the spaghetti to a saucepan of boiling water with a dash of salt. The salt will help the spaghetti have flavour. When al-dente (to the tooth), drain and set aside.

Whisk eggs, half of the cheese, Paprika and 2 tbsp of ground, black pepper into a mixing bowl, tipping the jamon Serrano mixture into it. Combine the hot pasta into the mixture, the heat of the pasta cooking

the eggs and leaving a creamy coating.
Season with salt and pepper, sprinkle the remaining
cheese and serve immediately.

I'll be the first to admit that I don't follow all the rules of *mise en place*; A French culinary term referring to all your ingredients being setup and prepared before cooking, as most of the time I'm making it up as I go along. However, this is a Spanish twist on the traditional Carbonara, although Mark would argue it needs cream and more cheese for his palate. If you're looking at moving to an off-grid property and you are yet to set up some form of electricity, then this recipe is not only delicious but budget friendly, and there's no need for a fridge.

CHAPTER 21

They say the first step on the road to recovery is acknowledging you have an addiction.

'Maybe it's time we gave it up, Abs,' Mark suggested. I hid my discontent by standing up, and answered calmly.

'No way! You're worse than I am! I'm not giving it up, not for anything.'

Mark walked out of the room. He glanced over his shoulder before grunting. We let it hang in there, not speaking to one another for the next hour. It wasn't spoken about until Monday morning.

That was how our discussion went last weekend. On Monday morning, without a word, we prepared ourselves for the 55km roundtrip into town. As the motorbike roared, we started our journey. The long roman road passed through low-lying plains. Fields and fields of flat land with a few groupings of trees adorned either side of the road. Passing through tiny villages the light breeze offered a slight respite from the seething heat, and our nostrils filled with the nauseating smell of manure. The odor of the tractors' operations is fortunately short-lived as it dissipates. It is a summertime tradition where farmers are spreading natural fertilizer over their land, whilst passer-goers would likely crinkle their noses at the smell, a lot of farmers don't mind it at all. In fact, one such old boy we spoke to said the smell was so ingrained, he almost liked it. 'Doesn't bother me at all, it's a sign we're going to get paid.' It's these times of year where the dry summer days where the dried crops have been removed, that the farmers can put their tractors to use and spread the manure that their animals have been piling up all year. Whilst I can appreciate the liquid gold, it hit me like one of Mark's dirty socks.

As we parked up, I whipped off my helmet, relieved the muffling wind turbulence had come to a stop. Even during the summer months, the supermarket was surprisingly quiet.

I can usually get away with camouflaging my nationality with my dyed, dark hair as nowadays although not common; it wasn't unheard of to see Spanish, blue-eyed and pale skinned women. Nevertheless, nothing said, *I'm English*, more than me walking through the aisles with a smile stretching from ear to ear and holding two boxes of PG Tips. I was so desperate for a cup of tea, I almost growled at the cashier. Because if I'm honest, I need at least two cups in the morning before I'm firing on all cylinders.

Even though where we were living I'd consider a few years behind the coast in the sense the area hadn't quite caught up with modernity, I can say for sure there are still parts of Spain so rural that the villagers had probably never even seen a car. But long gone are the days where tourists would have to bring over pounds of cheddar cheese and Cumberland sausages stuffed into their suitcases in pants and socks. Most supermarkets now stock at least a couple of British products, and on the coast you're bound to find an Iceland's supermarket somewhere. Moving inland meant our regular Mercadona was a good 55km roundtrip so we were pleased to find a Consum tucked between two village town houses in our local town, but when one Saturday morning the PG shelved displayed no boxes, Mark and I felt positively displeased, and they weren't likely to be re-stocking either. Instead, the cashier showed us another brand of tea four times the price with zero the taste. Her smile radiated as she picked up various boxes off the shelf, but I tried to convey to her it wasn't just about the taste, as I also love Earl Grey, but that PG always hits the spot. Nothing quite gets us going than a full-bodied builder's brew, and a chocolate digestive on the side. We left disappointed and dejected because there was nothing we could do. Instead we were subjected to another Spanish shrug.

Shocked and appalled, Mark expressed his aghast the entire trip home, and told me that I should be contacting the head of Consum with our despair, and that we will be joining other PG Tip supporters and that at least once a month we will be shopping in Mercadona which happened to be 25km away from Consum. I've rarely seen Mark so dismayed.

CHAPTER 22

*'Dear Mother Nature, please check the
thermostat, someone has set it to Hell,' Unknown*

August: It's been almost a year since we first viewed the house.

We had had a year of ups and downs, uncertainties and worries. But here we are, melting, learning new things every day. Today we discovered if we put our arm out of the car window, and felt so much as a cool breeze we were still in the 30s, if it felt like *why the fuck is the arm out of the vehicle, not inside, window up and A/C on, f&%$ing hot*, then we had reached the +40s. There were only certain times of the year where going faster just meant the hairdryer setting was on full. Even the little coves with turquoise water on the coast were too warm to enjoy at this time of the year. I remember one such beautiful coastal jewel had such a picturesque location that was ideal for snorkeling. An esplanade for hikers alongside the crystalline shore, and with its small *Chiringuito* it also happened to be my first time trying *Horchata*.

Horchata. Originated in North Africa, this white plant-based beverage is made from dried, crushed, ground and sweetened Tiger nuts and was first brought to Spain in the 13th century by the Arabs.

The result is a sweet, sickly milk like drink usually accompanied with local pastries called Fartons; typical of the Valencian town of Alboraira. And if the name wasn't bad enough, these elongated, glazed, spongy sweets are made for dipping into your white, creamy Horchata…

However, although you can order Horchata all year round, its rich-in-nutrients make it ideal as a winter refreshment.

So, here we are unable to do much with the insufferable temperatures. We never had the desire for a swimming pool in Spain, much to everyone's amazement. Then again, we never felt the need to, especially working all hours. That was until now… However, living in the countryside meant swimming pools were not allowed, funny Spanish laws. Yet, the idea of a cocktail pool or Jacuzzi where we could dip our toe and pop some bubbly sounded ideal. Mark brainstormed and converted the old, black one thousand litre water container from round the back into a plunge pool by cutting the top off. We could call it a plunge pool because traditionally they're flat-bottomed and shallow, much like our container. Although, it didn't quite look like a typical plunge pool at some Grecian Villa, it would do the job. It's hard to imagine, but it was beautiful and the palette of soft pastel colours of the surrounding forest and rocky headland made it feel like paradise. Ingenuity is Mark's forte.

The old, sun-damaged container bulged at the sides. It sat on our driveway facing the public dirt track that ascended and ended at our house. By now, both Mark and I were as hot and tired as a meat roll in a kebab shop, so using our hosepipe, Mark huffed and puffed, sucking water from our internal water deposit (ajibe) from a tube that exited the house sidewall, and dutifully it filled the container. The mere thought of wading in the water appeared to be the best idea Mark had had yet, a short respite from the ravenous mosquitoes that feasted on me throughout the day. I itched myself raw so much, it became an obsession, and I had to wipe the inner corners of my mouth because the scratching felt so good. I scurried off into the house, and grabbed two wine flutes and a chilled bottle of Cava; the one that had been in there for the last three months waiting for a special occasion. Upon returning, I saw Mark stark naked climbing four concrete blocks in an attempt to get inside the water container.

'Christ, Mark, if anyone comes up to the house they'll think a new species of Iberian Wolf has been discovered. Are you seriously going to go skinny dipping? What if someone drives up here and see's you?' I said laughing as I pulled on the cork.

'See's *us* you mean. Come on, strip off,' he smiled as he tapped the water as it spilled over the sides.

'Am I hell!' I scoffed. 'I'll be the lookout.'

However, Mark hopped out of the container and dragged me towards the water, clinging onto my arm in an effort to involve me in his comical antics.

'Come on, Abs, be free!'

The next few hours we sat in our plastic water container next to the public track, naked and unashamed watching the sun set. It wasn't quite the romantic Jacuzzi I envisioned but it did the job, even if I ended up wearing a tee-shirt because there just wasn't the room to have us both and a couple of floatation devices. I felt like we were on an episode of Naked and Afraid; an American reality TV series where two survivalists meet for the first time, and have to survive the harsh environment and dangerous wildlife in the wilderness naked. That's just what we needed, some Spanish Ibex ramming into us as we desperately grasped the sides. We had the hellscape, the relentless flies and mosquitos, so we were up for the challenge. We were just waiting for our monetary payoff from the reality TV show.

That evening, as we ascended the stairs, and switched on our old racketing fan, the bed sheets practically shimmered with thermal mirages. As Mark stripped off and climbed atop the duvet-less bed, I was once again reminded that the summer nights bring a loss of decorum. We both lay there spread eagled, the fan blowing hot air over our bodies, the heat, even at night so intense that rivulets of beaded sweat trickled off my face. As if the oppressive heat wasn't enough, I lay there wondering if the ghosts of the past were standing at the foot of our bed looking at this British couple sweating like two basted turkeys. I stared blindly into the dark up towards the ceiling, praying for sleep, and Mark groaned as he fell into a deep slumber. A faint light reflected through the window showing his arms and legs splayed like an angel, his naked, half dead mole-rat staring at me as if pleading to rescue it from the unrelenting heat.

Stop thinking about it and just take the plunge

CHAPTER 23

*Be with someone who loves you harder on days
you can't love yourself at all.*

Fortunately, temperatures like that are short-lived, and we can return to what some call living the dream, and others say surviving the nightmare. For us, it was a new life, a new start, and a new business. Because nothing ventured is nothing gained. Nevertheless, moving to rural Spain wasn't going to mean we would have any more luck in getting things done. Spain is known as having a nation of *mañana*-goers, as, why do today what you can put off tomorrow! Admittedly, it was and is always something both Mark and I struggle with. Not only being unconventional but darn right frustrating. However, as Anthony Bourdain once famously said, "Eat at a local restaurant tonight. Get the cream sauce. Have a cold pint at 4 o'clock in a mostly empty bar. Go somewhere you've never been. Listen to someone you think may have nothing in common with you. Order the steak rare. Eat an oyster. Have a negroni. Have two. Be open to a world where you may or may not understand or agree with the person next to you, but have a drink with them anyway. Eat slowly. Tip your server. Check in on your friends. Check in on yourself.

Enjoy the ride". So, that is precisely what we intend to do.

As we walked through our garden in the hottest time of the year, we could see the once green grass was now starting to yellow, without irrigation, it was unavoidable. It made a slight crunch as we walked through it, with sharp thistles standing proud and tall, stabbing into the side of our ankles. As we brushed against the drying fauna, our nostrils filled with an aromatic and succulent scent of terpenes. At the end of the garden was a grove of pine trees, their sharp yet sweet, sap oozing down the bark.

'Smelling airborne terpenes whilst walking through a pine forest is not unlike inhaling CBD oil, so they say,' Mark smiled.

'Oh, how wonderful... Isn't it unusual to have a cluster of pine trees among all these olive trees! It's our very own private wood.'

The loud, high-pitched whine of hundreds if not thousands of Cicadas shouting their mating call known as a chorus can be heard up to a mile away, and it provided the song of summer. However, despite the blinding heat, Mark and I raked up the ankle-twisting stones that erupted from the ground, a thankless task, and there were only so many hours we could dedicate to unadulterated sunshine before I, too ended up as overcooked and crispy, and bearing resemblance to Ghandi's flip-flop.

As we drove into town, we moosied through the

town square, sitting on one of the stone benches that adorned the water fall under the pergola. We watched as a couple of butterflies fluttered past us, their wings vibrant shades of red, white, and yellow. They wove in and out of the tree canopy, which was an assortment of native flora with impressive magnolia trees. I love how the Spanish take pride of their gardens and local personalities. In the city of Valencia itself, there is a small green space called Glorieta Gardens; it is home to monuments of famous Valencian natives such as a cast bronze bust that is dedicated to a painter Francisco Domingo. It boasts huge trees providing a relaxing space right in the heart of the city centre, and is located at the beginning of Colon Street, with the end next to *La Puerta de la Mar* the door to the sea. It's a park of historical significance dating back to 1812, a time of French occupation. The French general who was known as an amateur botanist began the garden and later it became known as La Glorieta Park. The large ficus trees are as old as 1852 and the latest facelift the park received was as far back as 1927.

As Mark and I sat quietly watching the water, a swarm of wasps began circling us. At first, I swatted, it appeared I angered them further. I stood up yelping and without a thought for Mark, ran to the nearest coffee shop. I barged through the swinging doors, gesticulating some rare form of sign language, and with my unorthodox entrance I attracted everyone's attention.

'Avispas!' I panted.

'Might as well grab a drink while we're here then, be rude not to.' Mark sighed as he followed suit.

I recalled the moment Mark and I were waiting for our laundry at the local laundrette. As we sat sipping coffee at a nearby coffee house, a distinct British accent caught our attention. Two couples were conversing with a Spanish lady in what can only be described as Spanglish. The conversation evolved around a dish that was recommended to the Spanish lady, 'You must try *patata asado* con Baked beans.' (Roast potato). The Spanish lady, intrigued, asked for clarification on the pronunciation of beans. The British man explained that it was indeed, 'beans', and that he and his wife were from Yorkshire. He then proceeded to reminisce about gravy, with his wife interrupting and fantasising about roast dinners and gravy. The Spanish lady nodded in agreement, and the couple added that sausages would be a great addition with the gravy. Mark and I refrained from looking as the Spanish lady stood up.

'*Bueno. Tengo que ir. Encantado,*' she said as she bid them farewell. As the Spanish lady left, the four of them continued their conversation.

'I thought she was a lesbian,' one of them remarked.

'Really? I thought she said she didn't like women, she only liked men,' another replied. The woman cackled and added, 'If she touched you, Mike, she would have to take you!' They all broke out into song.

'Touching me, touching you...aha.'

'Listen you two...'

'No!'

'What?'

'I'm not saying nuffin'.'

'Is it possible to get cuatro mas?' he asked pointing to his beer glass.

'You're ordering another?'

'Yeah.'

'Why?'

'Cos I sed so!'

I paid for our drinks and gave up around the time they were telling the waitress they didn't think much of Adele, claiming she moaned too much. What I took away from the experience was that, as a whole, us British really must try harder. I mean, come on, trying to persuade a Spanish lady that ham, egg and chips is a staple in one's diet and that Baked Beans should be on her list of British food to try. My face met the palm of my hand.

CHAPTER 24

'Life's like a bull race, and when you run with
bulls, you have to be ready for wounds.'
Ritesh Ranjan

How can Spain be dead and yet so alive in the month of August? With the sun blazing overhead, August is considered the hottest month of the year. The dry, yet humid insufferable torment gives many locals a reason to escape. However, August is the apex of the country's tourist season, with some of the wildest parties happening during the hottest time of year.

The weather is in full force, temperatures pushing 40 plus degrees Celsius, prices sky-rocket, foreigners get ripped-off, businesses close down, public officials, town halls, all collapse until September – after all, it is the time to party.

Gastronomic festivals celebrate and what were relatively ghost towns, now become alive. With the cities that never sleep, the bull running is the most eagerly awaited.

Throughout Spain, the event begins at the start of August after San Fermin that takes place in July. Historically, it's a festival of Pamplona so I heard, and Yesenia said they celebrated it here and in other parts of the country nonetheless. The bulls run every other day, and in between, the locals make fire pits that are erected from wood in the middle of the square, and large pots boil Gazpachá. Of course, making fire of any sorts is highly prohibited...unless it's a fiesta. With full stomachs and 40 plus degree Celcius, everyone is hot. From the young to the elderly, everyone commences in a water battle to cool off from the scorching sun. Spanish sure do like to party.

The running of the bulls can last for days or even a couple of weeks, and the town hall will spend thousands of Euros, and days prior to the running of the bulls constructing makeshift platforms consisting of large metal cages throughout each town.

The Spanish tradition is met with controversy, and since 2002, a new tradition has occurred The Running of the Nudes – supported by animal welfare groups such as PETA who object to the tradition claiming it cruel and how it glorifies bullfighting. Despite the outcry, the bull running continues and it has become a major tourism event. It was even performed in Stamford, rural England until 1837. The running of the bulls' origin began when cattle herders would transport their animals from the fields that border the cities where the animals were bred, through the towns to sell them at market or the bullring where they would be that evening's entertainment. During this process, youths and adults alike would run in a display of bravado to speed up the process by running between and in front of the cattle. And thus the tradition had begun.

As Mark and I sat in the town square that morning around 9:00 am, away from the raucous, nursing a lukewarm cup of coffee, the first rocket alerted us that the corral gate was open. The second rocket signaled that all the bulls had been released. *Encierro, (*the running of the bulls) had begun. We heard the screams as large and aggressive bulls ran through the town, youths flying in and out of the metal bars to escape being gored. Most runners are male but we did hear a couple of years ago an elderly lady had been caught up in the commotion and tragically passed away. It wasn't an event Mark nor myself, was interested in neither did we have a death wish, because we all know what happens when a wild animal is cornered.

Yesenia rang us, and seemingly appeared as light-headed and fruity as always. She said she would be joining us later on when she knew her father had returned safely from his jaunt up the mountain. Her father spent most of his time tending to his some two-hundred herd of goats and sheep, that ate everything in sight. Population in rural Spain is so vast that forest growth goes unchecked and contributes to forestall fires. By allowing ruminants to roam, not only sustains their dietary requirements but keeps the countryside trimmed as there are virtually no natural grazers. No herbivores equal fire.

However, with so many sheep, buying lamb is not one of the most widely consumed meats, and if you do find it in your local supermarket it rarely tastes like the lamb we've come to know. So don't be surprised if they give you goat or mutton at best. Instead, sheep are used for their milk, to produce cheese. One such cheese being Manchego cheese and it's made in the La Mancha area of Spain, specifically from the Manchega breed of sheep. Aged between 60 days and 2 years, this cheese preserves the medieval tradition of using basket-weave moulds and hard rinds. Ivory in colour, the flavour is nutty and buttery but firm and often enjoyed with various cured meats, wine and bread. I like to add a sprinkling of cumin to my sliced Manchego cheese just to add a little spice and an added kick.

Mark and I were headed towards Vega de Ayora Artisan Cheese Factory, who also owns a goat farm of Granadino-Murcian goat breed. The factory also is surrounded by 15,000m2 of oat, wheat and corn fields, and is what the goats are fed on. The cheeses are a natural and healthy artisanal product made by hand with 100% milk from their own herds, and are perfectly accompanied with a nice local wine.

CHAPTER 25

I'm not dead.

Not long after meeting Yenesia had she introduced us to a mirage of friends. One such friend, Rafa, being one, if not, the largest honey producer in the area. He sat opposite us, prising open salted sunflower seeds while he spoke, gesticulating and laughing out loud at Mark's lack of communicative skills. 'So,' he said. 'When do you want to visit the factory?' An invitation we couldn't refuse.

A day later we pulled up outside a large warehouse just outside town. Upon entering, immediately we were dumbstruck at the stacks and stacks of empty hives, and the rapid beating of bee wings. Rafa pulled back a large sliding door, where inside there were drums and drums, both full and empty adorning all four walls. Dead bee carcasses scattered on the floor.

'This is where the cream is stored, until we jar it,' Rafa explained.

'Cream?' Mark asked.

'Yes, cream. Honey cream. Here, taste some. This is Rosemary Honey Cream.'

Rafa yanked off the metal lid, inside there was a thick, white substance that looked like lard. He handed us both small plastic dippers, and gestured us to take a scoop. I never thought it was possible to taste the countryside through honey. Creamed honey is made from 100% pure honey in its raw form. It doesn't contain any cream or any other dairy ingredient despite its namesake. As we licked the creamy consistency off the dipper, we could taste the fine crystals, and Rafa explained that in an unpasteurized state, the honey wants to naturally harden, whilst pasteurised honey is runny and what we would typically find at the supermarket. If you love raw honey, I highly recommend giving honey cream a try. Apart from its impressive medicinal attributes, honey also has many anti-bacterial, anti-inflammatory and antioxidant properties as well as aiding in the treatment of gastrointestinal ailments.

The bee corpses continued as we wandered throughout the factory, Rafa said it was a normal part of the process with some several thousand bees dying as they transition from winter to spring. Winter bees are physiologically different than summer bees; they're fatter and designed to live longer. By contrast, summer bees only live for a few weeks. He didn't seem fazed by the abundance of bee carcasses because some worker bees are undertakers, cleaning the hives and surrounding areas of dead bodies. Sometimes the undertakers would drag bees that are still alive, barely, but not resisting, and carrying them up to 30ft away, Rafa's back yard being the defacto bee graveyard. It reminded me of Monty Pythons *"Bring Out Your Dead,"* when one of the so called dead slung over someone's shoulder says:

"I'm not dead."

"Here, he says he's not dead."

"Yes he is."

"I'm not."

"He isn't"

"Well, he will be very soon, he's very ill."

"I'm getting better."

"No you're not; you'll be stone dead in a moment."

I couldn't write about honey and Valencia without mentioning the Honey festival of Ayora that takes place every year in October. Ayora being the biggest Honey producer in the Valencian region, and the first cut *(El Primer Corte de La Miel)* being a huge annual celebration. Beginning as a beekeeping event, it has, over the years expanded, and is now a popular tourist attraction. Mark and I, as well as many other guests attended the fair which was divided into several areas around the Plaza Mayor, Glorieta and little side streets consisting of gastronomy, beekeeping, craft, shopping and more. We watched as bee keepers reproduced the honey process in a glass urn, opening our eyes into the process of honey making from start to finish – installing the hive to the extraction of honey.

The streets were beautifully decorated; plants,

flowers and with bees made out of different mediums. Side streets sold arts and crafts, with the main town devoted to gastronomy so we treated our palates to a variety of traditional flavours. Spain knows how to celebrate in style, and I find it amusing how they have strict rules for cutting down pine trees unless it's the townhall that does it. Then they can just plant 8 of them in the middle of the road, only to be removed after the festival.

A wonderful private tour around the honey factory

CHAPTER 26

Roses are red, mud is brown, 'round here we party
with the radio up and tailgate down.
Pinterest

'Where's the car key?' Mark panicked.

'It's in the drawer. Here,' I stated as I opened it and handed him the key.

'It belongs with the other keys if anything. That wouldn't be any good if you fell flat on your face and I couldn't find the key,' he remarked.

'Oh, is that the first thing you thought of, if I had an accident, and needed rushing to the hospital?' I smiled.

'Well, it's no good hiding it is there. What if you fell down the stairs and lay there unconscious. How would I go out and get something to eat?'

Mark took the key outside with him as he went to do his rounds of opening the car windows, as the weather although cooling, still reached the mid-thirties late morning, then he let the chickens out of their wooden house, whilst I gathered breakfast and a cup of tea.

One of the chickens was howling like a cockerel. We were unsure if it was her announcement to the world she was in labour and we were to come and collect her egg, or the excruciating pain. Eggatha, the white leghorn's average lay is around 60grams, twice delivering us a double yolker of 92grams.

Nonetheless, every morning, each hen was determined to ensure that, everyone knew they were awake, had laid and wanted out of their coop so they could run, wings slightly outstretched, head-bopping and feet thumping towards the dogs' empty bowls.

'I do not know why you are still grumpy, Mark. This is all you have ever wanted. We're living the dream.' I stared at Mark waiting for an answer. 'Well?' I continued.

'Yes, of course.'

'Then, what's the matter?'

'Just whether we are going to do all that is required without starving.'

'Hey, you and I have been through a lot worse! We can accomplish anything when we put our heads together. Did you get chook's egg?'

'I did. I've put it away.'

'Great. I thought we could go into town later on, do some shopping, and grab an ice-cream, at least before they shut up shop.'

Mark knew I was not talking about the small village in which we resided, but the town about 6km away where parking was somewhat of a nightmare at this time of year. Small Spanish villages are charming, but are not built for cars. Nonetheless, each village will celebrate some form or another depending on what that particular village is known for. Even if it means you walk for miles. Many villages we have visited offer a rosy-medieval hue with narrow, ancient cobbled stone streets, outstanding cathedrals, and sometimes cosy bars set inside caves. However, lost isn't part of the vocabulary when it comes to exploring Spanish villages. More often than not, you'll be able to enjoy them all year round without the raucous nature of tourism. If you enjoy hiking and isolation, take a trip to Asturias in northern Spain. There, you will find a small village with just 34 inhabitants and rewarded with spectacular views of the valley below. When we lived on the coast, we would frequently ride and head into the mountains into the gorgeous village Guadalest, although very busy during summer thanks to the day-trip from Benidorm. As a fortified village, and built during Spain's Moorish occupation in the 12th century, Guadalest is now a museum, having been partially destroyed by earthquakes. You will need a good pair of hiking boots to traipse and climb through the streets of Guadalest, but visiting the museum of torture where in its eleven rooms you can view more than 70 torture devices will make your hair stand on end. One of which, was used as a form of Capital Punishment right up to the mid-seventies.

We took our breakfast into the conservatory, and I heard a recognisable sound, a not too familiar sound, but one we recognised all too well; the sound of a small van charging up the dirt track that led to our house. Plumes of dust kicking out either side as it raced past our window. It was Juan. Not Juan as in Mark's friend from the flying club, but Juan, the old farmer. Behind him charged his two, panting dogs.

'What's he doing here at this time of the morning?' Mark snapped.

It wasn't that we had any problem with Juan, it's just we didn't want him around at 7:30 am. After a tumultuous start to our relationship, we realised it was just his nature to sound aggressive. Juan was an illiterate old farmer, known throughout our tiny village, and he couldn't see what the problem was allowing his dogs to free roam around our house – after all, they did so when he lived here. After the passing of his mother, and the reluctant sale of the house to the buyers before us, Juan had grown painfully bitter, because he wanted the house for himself, but when siblings are involved, it's not quite so simple. Traditionally, Spanish homes are passed down from one generation to the next, so with the family selling off only the house and its plot, not the surrounding farmland that stretched for hectares, meant Juan still popped up on occasion, and reminisced about happier times.

Fortunately, his dogs were pleasant, but we kept our animals inside nonetheless. The dogs, as loyal as they come waited patiently beside his car parked on his part of the countryside, and whilst he groaned to himself lopping off olive branches, he threw the larger of the two dogs a dried goat's leg to keep him entertained. I managed to sort out diplomatic relations by offering Juan some of our eggs, seeing as his hens were forcefully removed due to the second sale of the property to us, and he returned the gesture by banging on our door one evening yelling, 'H-O-L-A, A-B-B-A?' breathing heavily onto the glass. Upon me opening the door, he then shoved a cabbage into my arms. I guess we're friends now?

He had been brought up with the local mayor who now delivers our water; last time he joined us in the conservatory during a sudden downpour. We talked about chickens and how after just three days of having his, they had all been decapitated and drained of blood by *El hurón* – a ferret (or a Mongoose). Having a sanguivore amidst us was news to me.

Juan was also part of the village's oldest families; we later learnt that the whole town was formed from just six families so everyone knew everyone or were related. When you're a foreigner in a new town, it's always best to get along and eat humble pie. The smallest of Juan's dogs, Rambo, looked very much like a fully grown dog, but walked around on legs belonging to a Corgi, and he ran like a hot-dog on wheels. It would sit on the dirt track, tongue lolling out the side of its mouth.

Mark and I scooped in spoons of cornflakes as we watched. Too tempting not to, not that Juan did anything worth watching.

Of course, one would have to make certain concessions when moving to Spain. Whilst being fluent in the language isn't a necessity, it is appreciated and certainly helps. In rural Spain, many locals over the age of forty-five do not speak a word of English, and Spain's laidback attitude can mainly be down to them living in the wrong time zone. Restaurants are bustling when other countries are hanging up their chef jackets, and it all started back in 1940 when Spain's dictator General Francisco Franco decided to change Spain's time zone in solidarity with Nazi Germany. One such famous refugee that came to Spain was Otto Skorzeny who was an SS lieutenant colonel who commanded the Friedentahler unit. As an expert in espionage, the Americans nicknamed him *Caracortada,* Scarface, because of the large scars that furrowed his cheeks. Rescuing Italian dictator Benito Mussolini, earned him the title of "the most dangerous man in Europe", and he is believed to be one of the main organisers of ODESSA in Spain which was a secret organisation of former SS to help other SS members escape Germany to other countries where they might be safe such as South America. He once famously said to the Daily Express in 1952, "I finally feel free in Spain, I can remove my mask, and don't have any reasons to live in secret." Skorzeny died in Madrid in 1975.

Later that day, we had left Juan to attend his olive groves. Upon our return, we made light conversation; after all, what do we talk about?

'When is it going to rain, Juan?' I asked. I had fallen into that British custom of naturally talking about the weather during awkward silences.

'I'd like to know the answer to that myself. Not one olive this year,' he shook his head. 'And that's all over Spain.'

Olive oil had become a hot topic among the Spaniards. With the soaring heat and its devastating effects, with Spain now producing half its harvest compared to the year before. We could hear the tension in his voice.

'If we don't have any rain,' he continued, 'no one will buy it, it's just becoming too expensive. The drought has decimated our crops,' he huffed.

'We have olives on our trees, would you be interested in harvesting them this year and taking care of them?' I suggested in an effort for diplomatic relations.

'No,' Juan firmly snubbed.

Mark chimed in, 'What's he say?'

'I'll tell you after.'

Juan busied himself emptying the water butts around his small trees. His dogs, including his miniature Yorkie, sat patiently beside his van. *'Madre Mia…'* Juan grumbled as he picked his nose and gobbed on the floor, a habit that certainly puts my nose out of joint.

Few of our olive trees, *Olea europaea*, were bearing fruit. Although drought tolerant, the dry spells we had experienced early spring had affected the fruiting and flowering. I never considered myself much of a farmer, but there is a time, at least there was in ours, where futility had crept in. I wondered if it was a mid-life crisis when our daily rounds of working and having our own business had lost its charm, and we lost our vim and vigour. Certainly for Mark, he was finding life increasingly difficult; his knees needing a little more oiling, and his mind needing a little more stimulation. It was in these moments I had dreamt about our new life in the countryside, but harvesting olives certainly never crossed my mind.

We said our goodbyes to Juan, *'Adios!'* and made our way to our home.

'Well, we've done our bit,' I sighed.

'You couldn't invite him round for dinner could you? He'd be ringing one of the cat's necks thinking it was to go on the BBQ.'

'He's very rural that's for sure.'

'Rural.., that's one way of putting it.'

Juan's hostility was something we would have to accept, no doubt, his cantankerous behaviour brought on by the last vendors whom tore down his years of work of makeshift carports and fencing despite it failing to meet basic health and safety regulations. In his eyes, we were just crazy foreigners.

'Thank goodness that's the shopping over with.' At this time of year, our small village had become overrun with tourists; Mark calls them terrorists because of the carnage they cause, leaving their brains behind as they leisurely stroll in the roads completely oblivious to any traffic, and they glared at us as we edged slowly forward that disrupted their pathway. *'Oh piss off!'* Mark shouted as one had smacked the bonnet.

'The less we have to go out, the better!' And it wasn't just tourists Mark detested, it was cyclists too.

'You're not a people person are you, Mark?'

'No, it's not that. I just can't tolerate stupidity. I'm all for people enjoying themselves, and going on holiday, but more often than not, they're rude and obnoxious.'

That's why he installed an air horn on the Land Rover, as if the Land Rover wasn't big enough; we still had cars cutting us up on roundabouts, and cyclists undertaking us. However, a 129 decibel attachment should help solve the issue. Unfortunately, it gives Mark more gratification than one might have thought; taking great pleasure from sounding it whenever I walk towards the vehicle. My involuntary head-to-toe body spasm that impairs my self-control and the contortion of my face brings him to hysterics. I'm convinced it has brought on exclamation of sudden surprise where I experience sudden and involuntary bursts of profanity. It's either that or a symptom of a sleep disorder. One such customer who sneaked up and tapped me on the shoulder who was on the receiving end of my obscenities fortunately saw the humour in it and replied, "You only needed to ask!"

'When people are on holiday they forget other people aren't. Everyone's guilty of it,' I shrugged.

'Or they're just filthy, leaving their rubbish everywhere.'

'True. It's not much to ask, is it? To be mindful of others, and respect the country we're guests in.'

As we pulled up alongside our house, we could hear the chickens. I could see one chasing a sparrow around the coop; no doubt he had snuck in there for some water.

'All right, hang on.' I cooed as I unlatched the coop door.

All four sprinted over like mini Velociraptors and barged their way out, eagerly pecking at ants and grasshoppers. With their wings splayed they skipped along towards the back door, slowly the dog following behind. Mark walked through the house towards the kitchen, and as I opened the back door, all four hens and dog popped in, 'No, shoo, out. You, too Harley!' Mark herded. 'Oh, Eggatha's dropped one, Abbie.'

'What do you want me to do about it; I'm putting

the shopping away. Just grab some kitchen roll. Here,' I handed.

Mark bent down, his head pointing one way and his hand the other. As the tissue enveloped the poop, his face turned to disgust. 'AHH.'

'What?' I called.

'It's still warm.'

'For heaven's sake, it's just chicken poop!'

'And your dog has a huge tick by his penis.'

'Where? That's not a tick, it's a wart.' I laughed so loud.

'Oh, you just wait until your eyes start deteriorating. What's he doing in here anyway?' Mark grumbled.

My English Bulldog Harley had just turned 11. Struggling with the heat, he enjoyed lying on the cool floor tiles of the back room by the kitchen. If he were human, I would have taken a restraining order out by now because of his obsession with me. However, he wasn't aggressive with it, and he's never been any different since we rescued him from a backyard breeder near Madrid when he just turned 3. And the chickens, well, they too enjoyed following us around and pecking at wispy hairs on my legs. I'm even seriously thinking about throwing out my razor and epilator, the pain is the same, but at least one of us is enjoying themselves and getting something out of it.

If five years ago you had asked us where we thought we would live, and to make a list of things we thought we would be doing, then I can assure you that walking around on our very own country grounds, and analysing the differences between wild boar and Spanish ibex scat was not one of those listed. Nevertheless, if you do indeed find scat then rest assure if they're small, pea-sized pellets then they're more than likely rabbits. If they're pointed on one end, concaved the other, varying in shape, deposited in small piles and are about an inch / 3cm in size then they could belong to deer, Ibex and sheep. I need to get a new hobby.

How well do you know your animal poop?

CHAPTER 27

*"And with the sprig of a fruited olive, man is
purified in extreme health."*
Virgil, Aeneid

The sun still shone with a fierce ray despite the
reduction in temperature, and it beat down on me as
I made my way up to the olive trees. Some, the
more mature trees were heavy with fruit. I knew,
having seen Juan with his netting around the bases
of his, it was time to start the harvest. The air was
thick with a slightly sweet olive fragrance but also

like aniseed, and as I climbed the *bancales,* stepped plots of land with my shears in hand I thought about all the trees and the reality of it being worthwhile.

I laid a blue tarp around the base of the first tree, and I spent hours carefully pruning branches, and skinning others of their fruit. The olives landing on the tarp like hail stones as they dropped. Repeating the action, again and again, as I moved from one tree to the next, as I was determined to be able to grace our dining room table with our very own home-grown olives. Mark joined me shortly after, a chainsaw in tow.

'What are you going to do with that?' I asked.

'Cut branches.' He replied.

'Not with that, we're pruning not committing savagery. We do still want trees afterwards.'

Harvesting and pickling olives in a salt, water and lemon brine and waiting a few months for them to ferment is a labour of love, and it gave me a new appreciation for the weeks farmers would spend out in the groves. Admittedly, I didn't manage more than a few trees, because whilst we were fettling with improving our olive production, we acknowledged we had settled in to a *mañana* procrastinating routine that had been brought on by the severe weather.

'It will be interesting to see if the roof leaks after all that hard work,' Mark wondered, pointing to the inside of one of our outbuildings he was currently using as his workshop.

'I'll be damned if we have to remove the *tejas* the curved terracotta roof tiles, again.'

We resealed the concrete roof but we didn't replace it. Mark said it was common in Spain to have fissures and cracks in Spanish homes due to the extreme heat of summer and the contraction of the colder nights in winter, and in the outbuilding it wouldn't have been worthwhile to replace it.

This week, Mark had purchased a secondhand Pasquali tractor and matching trailer from Yesenia's father. It was all he talked about – excited he had another motor to add to his collection. With it being red and yellow - the colours of the Spanish flag, the old tractor would do the job of collecting all the lopped olive branches and bringing them to our drying pile until the weather permitted us to legally have a fire.

'Come on, Abs, have a go!' Mark suggested.

'OK!' *How hard can it be?* I thought.

Each level of our land is relatively flat so it hadn't occurred to me that I could be one of those hilarious tractor fails that drives a tractor into a ditch, or under bridges instead of over them and with Mark's deft hand to ensure I wouldn't cause more destruction than the tractor was made for, I thought, what could possible go wrong? With only 14hp I wasn't going anywhere in a rush.

'Just stay in a straight line and you will be fine,' Mark assured. Suffice to say, it drove just like a car; clutch on the left with a cable going towards the engine, brake in the middle with two cables going to the back axle.

However, it didn't stop Mark yelling at me from 100 yards away shouting 'BRAKE left …the other left.'

I didn't know it at the time, but Mark had plans for the top level of land, that being to create himself a runway for his RC planes. Because, you know, what Mark wants, Mark gets. I spent the next couple of days acting as a counter weight whilst he used the Land Rover to compact the land, like I'd make much difference to the two-tonne vehicle.

CHAPTER 28

*"I tell you, we are here on Earth to **fart around**,
and don't let anybody tell you different."*
Kurt Vonnegut

Sheila and her younger boyfriend came to visit us and stay for a couple of days. During their stay, we had a BBQ breakfast and sat around the stone table that Mark and I two weeks before had spent a few hours centralising and concreting into place. It was quite the ordeal, a reminder of me saying and instructing Mark to move it ever so slightly; 'Left a bit, no, too much…' and him getting infuriated with me. Us both disputing what we were centralising to. Eventually, after demanding I "get off my arse" he agreed to a spot situated between two trees.

Sheila and I sat around this darn table, and Sheila leant back, causing the bench to detach from its cement base. She rolled onto the ground like a commando on their first day of boot camp learning how to roll. Her expulsion of gas always tickled me, and the more she laughed, the more she farted. As Mark and Sheila's boyfriend joined us, they quickly put down their plates, grabbed her arms, and hoisted her back onto the stone bench. She was still laughing, and we thanked our lucky stars she was wearing a two-piece pajama set.

'It was the beans!' she proclaimed.

'Somehow I don't think it was the beans…' Mark mumbled.

In just two days, Sheila managed to make her new boyfriend's jaw drop more times than I could count. One of her more memorable moments was when she gave us a rather graphic demonstration of how her gynecologist had shown her how to apply vaginal cream. In addition, her friend Maria then told all her friends that she had seen Sheila's minky.

Mark was puzzled by the couple's apparent lack of common interests, and wondered why they were together. I suggested, it might very well be because he used to own an English bulldog. He had told me so when my Harley reminded him of his own canine friend that he owned before he moved to Spain.

In that case, he was used to flatulence as it was a common trait among Bulldogs. Harley was definitely Sheila's grandson, it was just opportunity before I captured them both tumble farting. However, the subject didn't stop there, because that evening Sheila chimed in saying that she didn't fart that much anymore, although, she did this morning, but that was the first time in a long time. Besides, if you fart you were healthy. Even when we changed the subject to Spanish cuisine, Sheila continued to talk about her bowel movements and how, when she was married to a Hungarian, her mother-in-law's dish of pig brain stew had given her flatulence all evening. She even joked that she had been "farting her brains out."

'It's a pity that you couldn't stay longer. It would have been wonderful for you both to meet The Booby Brothers.'

During our visit last week, when they graciously invited us round for dinner, we were amazed by the exotic wildlife that surrounded us, which was vastly different from what we are used to here. As we gazed up at the sky, an eagle soared overhead, its high-pitched scream alerting us to its presence. We also witnessed the breeding season of the red deer, and as expected, their resonant roars echoed far and wide. As we transition into early winter, the stags call out to compete for the attention of the hinds. The brothers informed us if we were lucky we would see a couple of deer on the way home, but alas we didn't. This is the difference between being surrounded by olive groves or thick dense pine forest.

We were lucky that morning, the morning Sheila and her boyfriend came to visit. The weather had forecast torrential rain. One moment we're outside sitting under the glaring rays and the next, the ground is engulfed in inches of rainfall. The water was a welcomed magic potion for the thirsty vegetation. I love the rain; precipitations are very irregular with only an average yearly rainfall in the Valencian region of 427mm or 16.8 inches, in Almeria, home to Europe's only semi-desert they have an average of 130mm per year. Compare that to the UK's average of 869.59mm from 1991-2020 and you learn to enjoy the rain.

CHAPTER 29

08:00 am Friday morning.
5 missed calls. 3 messages.

08:00 The Booby Brothers: 'Hey, we are going to Valencia, care to join?'
08:02 The Booby Brothers: 'You need a day off.'
08:07 The Booby Brothers: 'Stop sleeping!'
Missed voice call at 08:52

Valencia City

In less than an hour, Mark and I had finished up our morning chores and met up with The Booby Brothers and their mother. We all piled into their Opel Vivaro and drove for an hour and a half towards Valencia City. Mark and I had never been to this part of Valencia before: the large industrial side 5km from the city, so we were excited to explore. We stopped in a small municipality called Alfafar that has a total size of 10.1 km2 to grab something to eat. Asador CityWok, an all-you-can-eat Asian Kitchen, was our choice of restaurant that offered a wide variety of dishes, including artisanal pizzas, Valencian Paella (with snails), Argentinean grill, Mediterranean seafood, sushi and more for the reasonable price of €16.50.

During our meal, I was fascinated by the sight of a

shopping trolley of frozen meat, right there for us all to see and the robot waiter that seemed to know table numbers and deliver food. As it whizzed past us, it accidentally dropped a prawn on the floor. I half-expected a robotic arm to slip out from underneath it and dutifully sweep it up, but I was disappointed as it left the prawn behind. Cleaning up messes was still the job of mere human waiters it appeared. As our drinks were delivered, I watched the lone prawn on the floor, while a large man, huffed and puffed as he walked past with a plate full of food and slipped on the prawn, falling to the ground. A waiter hurried over, and before he hauled the man up, he picked up the prawn before a lawsuit ensued.

After lunch, we drove three minutes around the corner to Leroy Merlin to purchase supplies for our exterior bathroom renovation including a new door. With a Taco Bell, Gino's, KFC, Burger King and Carl's Jr Bigger, Better California Burgers all competing next to one another, I wondered if I was still in Spain. We then visited Bauhaus and Obramat before returning to Leroy Merlin once again. With almost everything we needed in hand, we were ready to head home. It had been a long day filled with laughter, good food and great company.

On our way back home, we stopped just off the exit towards Masalavés at La Pausa Alberique, a roadside restaurant that will only be remembered for its stench of manure that permeated the air. Hordes of people stood outside holding their noses; I can only guess that it was emanating from a nearby field.

At the rear of our house, we were fortunate to have several outbuildings. These included a log store, a room with a sink and fireplace that I had envisioned as an ideal laundry room, another room that Mark is currently using as a workshop, and a building at the back of it via an internal door, which then led out onto our garden. This room previously used as an old slaughter house was perfect for an outdoor bathroom and possibly an en-suite to the workshop, whenever we had time to renovate it and convert it into guest quarters. Although it required more effort, Mark and I decided to replace the old, metal garden door that led out from this exterior soon-to-be bathroom since the location of it opened out onto our new BBQ area. Additionally, it was only 5ft 3 tall. Given the possibility of an unpleasant odour that can occur in bathrooms, we found it necessary to block the hole up, and move the door's location to the other side. The door also featured a sheet, about a foot long of corrugated metal that protruded the wall, a poor effort at weather stripping. As Mark employed his cutting grinder to remove it, the apprehension of someone scalping themselves or having their toupée caught on the sharp edge thankfully began to dissipate.

However, we were not the only individuals who were involved in massive renovations taking place.

A couple of days later, we met up with The Booby Brothers. They told us we had to visit friends of theirs, a couple whom they had bid farewell to on our last visit to their house as the couple collected a dozen fresh eggs laid by the brothers' hens.

The couple who had been residing in our village for the past three years had kindly invited us to view their townhouse, which was situated in the heart of our village. Wilma described it as a "must-see". As with many Spanish villages, parking spaces are scarce outside one's front door. Instead, narrow alleys adorned by properties often no wider than a few meters are butted up against one another. As we walked along the quaint cobblestone street, we arrived outside large, wooden doors with a brass knocker. Meike opened it, barefoot and with a broad smile, and guided us inside. We were met with the most astonishing transformation. Purchased in 2017 for a mere €2,500, they told us the story of how they had become acquainted with the villagers after visiting six years ago. After informing the mayor at the time that they planned on relocating to Uruguay, he imbued the idea of renovating a dilapidated old townhouse belonging to one of his family members and practically gifted it to them to encourage them to stay. So that's what they did. Their journey has uncovered some amazing ancient discoveries: knocking through a wall to find two large ceramic pots that are at least a couple of hundred years old, renovating the old wooden beams, polishing and refining the original flooring, and showing us the small courtyard that housed pigs, chickens, and goats on multiple levels that is gradually falling down. We cautiously stepped through, careful not to touch or nudge the delicate crumbling stone walls, aware of the various acro stands supporting walls whose only reason for not collapsing is reliant on a hundreds-of-year-old wooden beam eaten by woodworm. It was quite comical seeing a hardhat hanging nearby. Jon showed us where they have started renovations and explained how their architect had ascertained their house to be at least 400-500 years old and built by the Arabs simply by how the walls had been constructed. It seems that the Arabs used mud and small stones, while the Spanish used larger stones. It was only a quick visit, and how I wish we could have stayed longer to take pictures of the house that felt more like a museum.

It's not uncommon to see expats moving to Spain without a specific area in mind, drawn by the idea of restoring a ruin and the relaxed way of life. You might see villagers sitting outside on pavement until late hours, with their front door blinds pulled down to protect the indoors from heat or insects. You might also see odd planters adorning windowsills and sun-weathered men standing outside bars, cheerily playing cards with a beer and a cigarette. However, it's important to note that the property you view may not always be like that in the photographs. It's not uncommon to see images of someone's bathroom with their laundry spilling out, an unmade bed, or photographs of people eating at a table strategically positioned in front of a sofa near the fireplace.

I find it hard to imagine how this couple managed to survive their first year in Spain, let alone a winter. Similarly, I'm puzzled as to why the vendors of our house gave up and moved on after only three months. Perhaps it was the poorly rendered brick walls, the amateurish electrical installation or the whole poorly constructed property looking decidedly dangerous. Even the newly renovated built walls had begun to crack. Nevertheless, if you have a vision and a good imagination, anything is possible. An old animal corral can be transformed into a secret garden with a magical hidden oasis tucked away in the corner, where you can escape from the bustle of everyday life. A falling-down stone wall can become a feature that Bougainvillea can trail across. Where some would travel across the world to visit ancient ruins and age-old artifacts, others go to Spain and fall in love with a ruin, and in some cases it turns out to be a money pit.

CHAPTER 30

Christmas holidays at the Davies'

Sheila, as well as Philip and Winnie were joining us for dinner over the Christmas period. The Booby Brothers were popping over too. A time I thoroughly enjoyed as it was the occasion of celebration and we had a lot to celebrate. It was to be our first proper Christmas spent at the house, and our one year anniversary of living there.

The colder weather brought new discoveries. In search for a more reputable wild boar supplier, we travelled through Cofrentes; a town little more than a hundred kilometres from the city of Valencia. Cofrentes is the largest leisure destination in the region, and we were lucky to have it nearby. There is a cruise on the river Jucar, canoeing and rafting routes, there is a reservoir, a campsite called the field of the priest, a nuclear power plant and a volcano situated on the Agras hill that is estimated to be around 1-2.6 million years old. An agricultural tractor converted into a charming, little train called The Volcano train will take you on an hour and a half guided tour that will begin its journey at a spa and end up at the volcano where the remains of a volcanic cone 1,000 meters in diameter remain.

Skirting off the N330, we ascended 527 meters and accidently came across a group of people nestled amongst the mountains inside a large complex. They were glaring at us, and walking around in white robes like some kind of cult. We hadn't realised at the time that we had inadvertently discovered the Hervideros Spa where there can be seen an expulsion of CO_2 (carbon dioxide) and CH_4 (methane) through a magma chamber that releases bubbles towards the spa's spring which looks like boiling water but it's actually cold. I half expected the springs to be The Devil's Bean pot where, with the volcano, Satan himself cooked over the flames of hell and invited all his white-robed worshippers to join him by praying and chanting in the hills of Cofrentes. Of course, we could have it completely wrong; they might have been ethereal figures, or fans of The Lord of the Rings. We didn't stick around to find out.

It led us to the discovery of the Volcan Cerro de Agras. You wouldn't know it was there unless someone had told you, Spain isn't known for having great signage. We ascended up the dirt track towards the crater, passing falling black lava rock known as basalt; an igneous rock that forms when molten lava cools and solidifies.

After parking up, at the edge of the crater, we could see the large volcanic bomb sat proudly in the middle of an esplanade of lapilli – latin for little red lava stones, and is material from 2-64mm that had fallen from the air during an eruption. The volcano is known as a strombolian volcano, where its eruptions were discrete, explosive bursts that ejected pyroclasts as high as hundreds of feet into the air in firework-like incandescent fountaining of liquid lava. Fortunately, the volcano lies dormant, but evidence of landslides are a reminder of what happened.

The volcanic bomb

Our trip out hadn't been a wasted effort in our search for the elusive butcher. A whisper here and there led us to a local butcher, who can supply wild boar without the ominous rendezvousing in a dark alley with Pedro. Armed with just a number, I texted him our requirements and the response was anything other than expected.

'Quien eres?' who are you? He replied.

Here we go again.

'Tengo ciervo,' I have venison, he pushed.

'But I don't want venison, I want boar.'

'Pues, puedo matar uno…' well, I can kill one.

I looked at Mark. 'I think it's best we go and introduce ourselves in person.'

I don't know what I expected, perhaps a white apron with red stripes to minimise the appearance of blood stains. He was a big, stout man with a florid face and a missing front tooth. His apron was white but not clean, and a large belt hung around his waist. Sides of meat hung from large impressive hooks, one above a round wooden chopping board with a central dip from years of hacking. We arrived as he was filling a large cylinder with meat, then he placed a skin over the nozzle and started turning the handle. Both Mark and I just watched as the emerging sausage entered his hand, and with a quick twist an individual sausage was made before the next.

'Hola!' he grinned.

'Hola!'

I noticed there wasn't any ready-made mince, but a mincer beside him. Some say, back in the old days mince meat was suspect, not knowing what went into it. It was refreshing to see that this butcher allowed customers to choose their fresh meat and have it minced in front of them and nothing was concealed.

It isn't a surprise that Spain's approach to food in some aspects is still very much of the middle ages with many of its characteristic flavours meeting that of the north African palate, with moors having brought saffron, coriander, fresh fruits and nuts, and so on that are widely used particularly almonds, in savory dishes. The festival of Moros y Cristianos is a spectacle of colour and tradition that has been celebrated for hundreds of years. And if you ever spend time in Spain during these festivities then you'll enjoy a theatrical performance commemorating the battle of the Reconquista. The streets are filled with parades, animals such as camels and horses, gunpowder and cavalry, loud music and eccentric costumes. It was and still is a time of great importance, and it's evident with its cobble stoned streets, wrought-iron balconies, castles, arched stone buildings being all very well preserved. Their annual fiestas bringing to the forefront of their medieval heritage, and in most towns you can choose which camp to reside in by mingling with those of your own nationality and language or not because in Spain you can have and eat the proverbial cake from one day to the next.

It sounds almost unheard of in today's society that the population of an entire village may not only have been born there, were raised there and had never left. We know such man who is 69 years of age, born and bred in the town of Benissa. It would take you half an hour just to walk a few hundred yards because everyone would be stopping and greeting him as if they hadn't seen one another for months. The outside world to some village folk is a place of fear, and change and I can understand that to some extent. In some aspects some older village people still live life as that of their ancestors with much influence from the Moors being a term referred to anyone of Arabic decent. In the south west of Valencia there is a human cave painting depicting a figure clinging tightly to a vine as they reach across into a bee's nest. Bees hovering obviously dismayed by the intruder, and it reminded me of their very hands on approach to sourcing food.

Every year hundreds of people converge to attend a medieval market filling streets within the town. The fragrant oriental spices wafting through the air blend with the range of local produce and like back in the old days, no fridge or wash facilities are in sight. Stallholders will dress in traditional medieval wear and will sell anything you can imagine from cheese to donkeys, so if you want to go back in time to combine both culture and celebration then don't miss out. Live puppeteers and battle re-enactments are also common in some areas. If you have a strong stomach, try everything on offer, there are plenty of samples to go around.

It wasn't long before the butcher had completed his string of sausages, tying them up neatly and slinging them over one of the hanging hooks. And whilst we waited we looked at the walls that were decorated with a black and white image of he himself slaughtering a large pig, taxidermy heads of a bull, Spanish Ibex, deer as well as a couple of stuffed pigeons with numerous trophies. This was a proud butcher shop with big, bold lettering advertising the meat is owned and grown locally.

After an introduction, placing our order and a half hour chat he asked us if we were going to attend *La Matanza*. This was something I had never heard of, but with the word *matar* meaning to kill in the name I didn't think it was about stroking fluffy bunny rabbits.

A couple of weeks later I awoke to the ping of my phone. At 3:00 am, I opened to a photograph of two large boars lay on the floor of his butcher shop. A few minutes later, they were prepped with the caption, 'It's here when you're ready.'

'Oh, Jesus…' I showed Mark the next morning. 'I'm not sure how I feel about this. I'm so conflicted.'

We dropped in to the shop, and he waved me through. Mark stayed out the front, and although I waited for him to join me, the butcher insisted I followed him towards the freezers. There, he whipped off a towel revealing the semi-frozen dissected joints of meat. He tugged and pulled them apart bagging what we had asked for, and then decided that, as they had been so lucky in their hunt, I was going to get two hogs for the price of one.

I walked out of the back room carrying the large bags, and he patted me on the back of the shoulder with his bloodied hand. *Great…* and I cringed at the thought of a bloodied handprint creeping onto my shoulder like I had managed to escape the clutches of a serial killer. But at least that's Christmas dinner sorted.

Our dining room was adorned with the festive cheer after I had spent hours erecting the large tree. This year, we could plug in our Christmas lights so it perfectly captured the essence of the holiday period. Our long, dining table and the over-hanging wagon wheel light gave it a touch of ancient medieval charm, and I looked forward to my guests for the first time, in my own home, enjoying the feast I was about to prepare. It was a sight to behold. Mark, although bah humbug had made an impressive wreath that sat in the centre of the table consisting of pine cones from our copse of pine trees, and small olive branches; the pliable nature bending them into a perfect sphere. As the guests arrived, the room was bathed with a soft, yellow glow. The room smelt of *Glühwein* – a tradition I grew up with that always evoked the smell of Christmas with its cinnamon, and deep, citrus, spices and ginger.

'I'm a bit worried…' Wilma stated as I poured everyone a glass.

'Why?' I laughed.

'Because you write about serial killers, have a freezer full of boar meat. Cas just told me you bought that industrial mincer off Bill, and I saw a huge meat tenderizer out the back,' he voiced.

'Hmm. I did wonder myself what I was going to do with it all. Don't worry, there is no taboo delicacy being served tonight,' I nodded.

'Boar?' Winnie cried.

'Yep,' Mark assured.

'Oh no…' she continued. 'Philip showed me those photos, I can't eat that.'

'But you eat pork, beef, chicken etc…' Philip raised his brows. 'What's the problem?'

'Boars are decimating the Spanish countryside. The pig population is causing chaos. Just try it. It's lean, and full of flavour. Abs cooks it wonderfully,' Mark exclaimed.

'Thank you, Mark.'

I'd marinated the tenderloin in olive oil, salt and pepper, lots of lime juice and fresh, ground chilli powder. With the meat being so lean, I relied on the acidity of the lime to help tenderise it by breaking down the protein. It makes it more palatable if you're not intending to cook it for hours on end. It was to be the centerpiece of our Christmas feast. I also relished the anticipation of savouring my garlic-roasted potatoes. They were delightfully airy and fluffy, with a crisp, golden exterior. I took great pleasure in knowing that they were the first harvest from my rubber bucket.

I love how everything is sourced locally. Even the rosemary is plucked from our own back garden, the potatoes, all my protein, the olive oil and even the wine, all sourced either from my garden or in and around the town we reside.

I chose not to disclose the origin and the events that unfolded of the wild boar to my guests, because I am convinced that the butcher is a sadist. However, he also provided us with venison. When Mark went to collect it, he was escorted to the back room where he witnessed something that I can only imagine. Mark expressed his interest in obtaining the antlers, possibly for the purpose of creating a cyborg; a twist on our fondness for all things Star Trek. However, the butcher failed to comprehend his request, so the both of us once again went in to the shop, to which the butcher emerged with the deer's head.

'That's just not right!' I exclaimed.

The butcher let out a chuckle. 'It seems she's a bit sensitive, isn't she?'

CHAPTER 31

Not all those that wander are lost.

Mark reckons riding motorcycles in 43 degree Celcius is as fun as dipping his willy in a hot bowl of soup.

So, we capitalised on the favourable weather conditions and embarked on a motorcycle journey to Cortes de Pallas. We had heard it was a beautiful place and picturesque it was. The town is nestled in the province of Valencia, the Jucar River carefully carves through the region, forming a canyon that serves as a reservoir for El Naranjero and Cortes-La Muela. During the night, the Cofrentes thermonuclear power plant harnesses its surplus energy production to pump water into the Cortes-La Muela reservoir, thereby generating clean energy during the day.

To reach Cortes de Pallas, we traversed the N330, passing through Cofrentes before joining the CV428. Upon arrival, I heard the faint chitter-chatter of an elderly woman, and as I approached her, I inquired about the traditional culinary delights of the village. She promptly recommended Gacha, a dish synonymous with Porridge, although I had only ever heard the word mean mush. This hearty mountain meal is cherished by locals due to the region's harsh winters, and I can imagine snuggling on the sofa on a cold, rainy day with a bowl of "mush" with a drizzle of honey to soothe the soul. Notably, Gachamiga is another popular dish in Cortes de Pallas as well as in Villena, Yecla, Hoya de Castalla, and numerous other regions.

Curiosity peaked; I sought further clarification regarding the key ingredients that constituted a delectable Gachamiga. It appears flour, garlic, water, oil, and salt are fundamental components of this dish. Perhaps one day I will attempt to recreate it. However, I remain sceptical as to whether these dishes prepared in the way described in this enchanting town will captivate my discerning palate.

Cortes de Pallas is home to approximately 800 inhabitants and boasts an architectural landscape reminiscent of its medieval origins. Narrow streets took us to steep slopes that characterise this charming town that has stood the test of time. However, it was the breathtaking scenery that truly left us an indelible impression. Nature enthusiasts and water sport aficionados would easily find solace here. Additionally, we learnt there was a captivating cave in close proximity to the Chirel Castle that would have you ducking and diving, marvelling at the bats soaring overhead.

Traversing the roads in and around our local town can often take us far and wide, sometimes leading us down paths better suited for adventure motorcycles. Yesterday, our journey took us into the Albacete province that borders with Valencia, where the stunning French-like countryside is reminiscent of the Serengeti. Here, the phrase "The place where the land runs forever" truly comes to life, evoking vivid images of the savanna with its crisp, golden grasslands and majestic, solitary trees. In addition, it shares similar undulating woodland, where towering pines replace the usual scattered Acacia trees. One might even mistake a Spanish Ibex for a Gazelle. Fortunately, vexing hyenas and hungry lions are not likely to cross your path. Although that wouldn't seem totally insane seeing as Duncan takes care of the lions for the Lion Man.

I was convinced he was pulling my leg when he mentioned he had to dash off to procure chicken carcasses for the lions. As it turns out, his neighbour is the proud owner of three lions, having spent several years in the circus industry. Nowadays, even at seventy-six years of age, he shuttles between Africa, the UK and his hometown for undisclosed business reasons. The lions freely wander around an enclosed area on his estate, gradually growing older and passing away. There were whispers that he even had an elephant and other exotic animals in his possession.

It's not just the scenery that is reminiscent of Africa. Spain and North Africa have quite the tumultuous relationship, as we learnt when we were looking at going 4x4 in Morocco. The North

African influence is more evident the further inland or south you travel. Take Granada for example, both a city and province in Andalusia is world-famous for its Moorish architecture and history, the Alhambra being the crown jewel of Islamic Art. The Alhambra, a palace and fortress complex was once a self-contained city that separated itself from the rest of Granada below. It is one of the best preserved palaces of the historic Islamic world, and you can reach Tangier from Granada in less than 400km.

Spain's countryside boasts a remarkable diversity that has enabled it to depict the arid highlands of Afghanistan in director Guy Ritchie's The Covenant. Sax and Villajoyosa, two barren and remote areas near Alicante, were chosen to emulate the Afghan landscape. George RR Martin, the author of A Song of Ice and Fire, which inspired Game of Thrones and House of the Dragon, said that the Moorish parts of Spain were a source of inspiration for his creation of the Kingdom of Dorne. Some of the Spanish locations that featured in Game of Thrones are:

Peñíscola – The coastal town in Valencia which was used for Meereen scenes, where Daenerys Targaryen tries to free her slave army.

Seville, Girona, Almeria, Zafra Castle, Cáceres, Gaztelugatxe and Cordoba among others.

I wondered whether, in this locale's backwoods, we would encounter the Sahara sandstorms to the same degree as we did on the coast. The airborne dust would tinge the heavens with an orange-hue, an apocalyptic spectacle for those who have yet to witness it. On numerous occasions, I have awoken to a surreal sky filled with minuscule particles of dust that had traversed thousands of miles across the Mediterranean seas, blanketing everything in a layer of red silt, which Mark found quite bothersome as we both spent the next hour cleaning it up.

CHAPTER 32

"Every country gets the circus it deserves."
Erica Jong

La Matanza festival – the slaughter of the pig; I came to learn is a dying old-age way of Spanish surviving the winter months. It is an ancient ritual that has garnered new interest as foodies are becoming more passionate about where their food comes from and how it is raised. Some tourists are now being allowed to attend the event, and witness the whole process that takes place over a period of three days, starting with the actual slaughtering of the pig. It's a sustainable way of living, with lots of cooking and copious amount of drinking.

Free-range, organic eating has been the norm for centuries in Spain, and in the *dehesa;* a landscape of grassland used for grazing animals, people are now able to learn about the relationship between food and where it comes from.

I shook my head in response to knowing about *La Matanza*, it was one of many traditions of Spain I hadn't even heard of, especially on coastal Spain. The butcher smiled broadly and clapped his hands together, said we must go and we would be his special guests.

It wasn't something neither Mark nor myself would voluntarily want to witness, but having spoken to the estate agent who has not only lived around here in the area for some fifteen years, she is also a vegetarian. She too, had been invited to a *Matanza* and lived to tell the tale. Without giving too much away, she did tell us it was something worth going to if we had the opportunity to, because it is important to know where our food comes from, even if the experience is unpleasant, to put it lightly.

On the day we could see it was an intimate affair. If there were any other foreigners, we didn't know about it. Instead, we watched in silence like voyeurs. We weren't looking for that visceral experience; we were just there out of politeness, not really knowing where to stand or who to speak to. Everyone was happy, cheering one another, patting each other on the backs as they sharpened knives. The matriarchal women wore aprons, and lined up next to each other along tables, cutting and chopping vegetables. The butcher had carefully spoken about the tradition; I'd also done a little bit of research beforehand as to be respectful. It was an honour we had the opportunity to witness their rural tradition even if to modern man it appeared a bit backward. We weren't far from the town itself, and one farmer walked towards the town square, behind him tethered to his hand was the pig. Other farmers stroked it and spoke to it softly. A couple of women stood to the side with rubber buckets, and in less than half a minute, the animal had met with the farmer and his knife wielding hand. The women hurriedly placed their buckets underneath the animal to collect the blood.

'Ven aqui,' our butcher waved, as he asked us to join him. Now, it was down to the women. The animal is then covered in straw and burnt over a low charcoal fire; this removes any hair and debris. The butcher helped hoister the animal up onto a metal contraption, and as they disemboweled it, we followed the women to the garage, where we saw ham joints curing from last year. Here, there was also a recently butchered goat. This was to be served for lunch. The older woman, Paula, mixed onions, vinegar and other ingredients into her boiling pot, whilst she mixed the contents of her bucket with oats and spices.

'Te gusta morcilla?' one elderly woman smiled and asked if we liked black pudding, and before I had chance to answer, Mark saved the day and interjected with his customary, *'Si si!'* Only now did we understand the story behind the butcher's photograph proudly displayed inside his shop. Whilst the music blasted from townhouses, children danced. It certainly opened our eyes, and it was if anything good to see that nothing went to waste from literally nose to tail. Perhaps Spain and its ancient traditions were worth saving and learning from after all, because Spanish don't waste anything.

Naturally, in Spain, lunch would be incomplete without wine. Mark and I decided to express our gratitude and leave the family to their affairs. There was something about the day's events that made us lose our appetites. On our way back home, we pondered over why this tradition still existed, albeit very rare, and I recollected how Paula and one of her acquaintances had discussed their fondness for consuming what they had produced, emphasising that it wouldn't taste the same if it was purchased from a supermarket. They were aware and conscious that their animals had led a contented and healthy life. That I understood. Isn't this the very reason more and more people are moving to a lifestyle without the reliance of public utilities? To live a life where you're self-sufficient or perhaps seeking to reduce environmental impact or your carbon footprint so to speak? Is this not the same reason so many of us have backyard chickens and collect our freshly laid eggs every morning?

Because, by reducing the cost of living by growing and consuming food that is fresh, healthy and free from harmful chemicals is ensuring it is of the highest quality.

CHAPTER 33

*If we wait until we're ready, we will be waiting
for the rest of our lives.*

If someone had asked me two decades ago where I envisioned myself in twenty years, and whether I could fathom the idea of remaining in Spain, I would have laughed and replied, "I hope not!" At that juncture, I had reached my limit. However, even though I'd had enough, I had barely scratched the surface of what Spain had to offer. I am grateful that I am still here. As I have previously stated, does one unfavourable chapter represent the end of the story? Certainly not! Because every one of us are the protagonists of our own narrative and you are penning it every day.

Bumping into Mark was a fortuitous turn of events, a blessing in disguise if I'm honest. I believe we complement each other, and occasionally, when he's in the right mood, he will admit to that as well. We are like two sides of a coin or two peas in a pod. Therefore, when we both harboured the dream of relocating to the countryside, it became an objective we were determined to achieve.

Homesteading does not necessarily guarantee good health. However, acquiring the skill set to survive self-sufficiently or at least partially self-sufficiently and actively engaging with your land can contribute to overall well-being and happiness. Undoubtedly, our move to rural Spain has been beneficial. We now suffer with very few migraines, if any at all. My asthma has virtually vanished. Moreover, it affords us the opportunity to revel the great outdoors without venturing far from home.

Our stress levels have diminished, our happiness has flourished, and our energy levels have soared.

The thick mountainous regions have a certain allure that enhances both physical and mental well-being. Furthermore, the elevated altitude has given us the privacy we yearned for, creating a relaxing, living space. Perhaps we will even take up yodelling.

Ensuring that we reside in a beautiful world with freedom and the abundance of fresh food has not been an easy endeavor. Friends and family deemed us mad, and financially reckless, while others commended our bravery. However, in all honesty, it's none of the aforementioned; it is simply forging ahead, getting on and pursuing our goal without waiting for the "When the time is right", because such a time never truly arrives. It's never the right time.

Here in the western part of the Valencian community, we have access to a variety of locally produced goods. For instance, we can buy raw honey, organically grown fruit and vegetables from a local cooperative. Something I missed back on the coast. If there was a cooperative, I never knew about it. The olive oil available here is farm-to-table and has no need for pesticides. The olives have been growing here for generations. If you have olive trees yourself, you can even bring your own olives to press, which in itself I would have thought is something hard to come by in the UK.

We have also made an effort to be more aware and value the welfare of the animals, because that is key to a superior product. We also make sure to purchase good quality meat, we have our own free-range eggs, and cheese is bought from a local cheese factory. Additionally we enjoy using our wild, fresh herbs picked from our garden and lemons right off the tree.

Recalling the curry recipe earlier, I continued to experiment with various spices and was pleasantly surprised with the outcome. I prepared a Daal Gosht, a North Indian curry that traditionally uses lamb and lentils. However, I substituted these two items with potatoes and broccoli to create another delectable vegan curry. Additionally, I prepared a Kofta curry, an Indian meatball curry. With our ample supply of wild boar, I created my own Moroccan and Indian inspired curry – a culinary feat I never thought I would be able to accomplish. Although seemingly insignificant in the grand scheme of things, it is testament to one's capabilities when they are compelled to act, even if it is merely to satiate our culinary cravings in a foreign country. Just don't expect me to be making my own tea.

We have recently started playing Padel, a sport that's gaining popularity in Spain. We play with the brothers and Wilma's ex-girlfriend and her current beau. His ex-girlfriend is an older Dutch lady who gets flustered much to Mark's amusement as they argue different score results. She also knew and had been victim to one of Duncan's attempted duncs. Mark claims that we're just flies in Wilma's sexual ointment at winding up the opposition, perhaps we are! *Ménage à Trois.* It breaks the week up.

Reflecting on our disastrous property viewings, we truly believe this house was chosen for us. Perhaps Mark's father was up there looking down on us from heaven helping to pave our way here. We sometimes imagine him walking around the garden, topless with a ciggy, just as he would have when he came out to visit. He would sit in the garden for hours on end, soaking up the rays. He would have loved it here.

So here's to you Vern, cheers!

Salut I Força al Canut!

"When the sun has set, no candle can replace it."
George R.R Martin.

ABOUT THE AUTHOR

E.J. Wood is a writer who resides in Spain with her family and a menagerie of animals.

She has a background in Business Marketing and, after running her own business for over 12 years, she is now restoring an old finca and exploring the Spanish countryside on her motorcycle.

E.J. enjoys reading about World War II and collecting memorabilia. Her novel, Amalie, was inspired by this interest and tells the story of a young girl who survives Auschwitz. In addition to writing, E.J. and her partner create movie memorabilia for themselves and others. Some items in their collection include a Predator helmet, an Alien skull, and a Star Trek Klingon Bat'leth.

E.J. is an unabashed cat lover, accepting her crazy cat lady title, and enjoys the smell of fresh laundry, writing, motorcycling, and cooking.

This is her first travelogue.

CONNECT WITH E.J. WOOD

www.Instagram.com/e_j_wood_author
www.Facebook.com/authorejwood
www.ejwoodauthor.com

If you're new to the works of E.J. Wood, why not read one of her crime novels? The Kidnapper's Word is book 1 in the DCI Landon series, featuring the impulsive, charming and eloquent detective Clarence Landon.

THE LOCATION

Sussex is a beautiful historic county that was created in the 5th century. It was formerly an independent medieval Anglo-saxon Kingdom, and is bounded by Hampshire, Surrey and Kent. Sussex played a key role in the conquest of Britain and significant signs of Roman presence can be found.

The whole of Sussex countryside is rich with fairytale castles and stately homes. Certainly a joyous experience for many tourists.

But there is a dark side to Sussex. Even the serene and tranquil Clapham Wood near Worthing has been known as one of the county's most haunted places with reports of UFO sightings, missing pets and Satanic Cult activity. Its reputation comes of no surprise with the amount of bodies that continue to be found.

ABOUT THE BOOK

Meet Clarence Landon, Detective Chief Inspector working for the Sussex Police force during the 1960s. Unsurpassed in his intelligence, Clarence is a renowned officer of the law and has a natural instinct for understanding the criminal mind. But is it enough to solve a case that is a little too close to home?

When nine year old Emily disappears, Detective Chief Inspector Clarence Landon knows time isn't on his side.

It's the 1960s. Child abductions are rare. Her mother, Ava blames herself. What mother would leave their child alone?

Behind twitching curtains, an unsettling truth of what happened is revealed. A story of family secrets and a chilling tale of deception is unraveled.

What would you be capable of when pushed to your limits?

BUY HERE ON AMAZON

https://www.amazon.co.uk/gp/product/B09HSC2 FVR

BIBLIOGRAPHY
Lock, Stock and Two Smoking Paellas

https://www.britannica.com/place/Al-Andalus

https://veryvalencia.com/things-to-do/attractions/parks-gardens-and-bridges/366-glorieta-gardens

Paella Facts: 20 Things to Know Before You Order (travelersuniverse.com)

Food History Friday: The Moorish influence on Spain's culinary history

POSTED ON JULY 5, 2013 BY SARAH

Food History Friday: The Moorish influence on Spain's culinary history | Travel Fare (wordpress.com)

Climate of the United Kingdom – Wikipedia.